Public Speaking Without Throwing Up

How to Develop Confidence, Influence People, and Overcome Anxiety

By: Dana Williams

Table of Contents

Introduction

At some point in our lives, we may have dreamed of being huge successes. We imagine being cheered on, loved, and respected by those around us. On the other hand, we worry about what others will think if we make a mistake. It can be scary getting up in front of others and being watched, but it can be so much more rewarding than it is scary.

The ability to touch someone's life is a beautiful thing. We all have one life, and we all have experiences that make it up. What you say could change the entire direction of someone's life. A person attends a real-estate seminar and decides to be a realtor. An addict attends a preaching service and decides to stop their habits.

Anyone can be influential. You don't have to be a top CEO. Sometimes people are influential without meaning to be. A lot of times the things we say can stick around in the minds of others for a long time.

Our words can provoke emotions in others. When we say something that brings out an emotion, people are more likely to remember what you said. They remember how they feel about something.

Emotion triggers parts of our brain that involve memory and connection. Emotions can act as a strong motivator when it comes to remembering something. When information travels from the short-term memory to the long-term memory, our listeners are going to be able to recall that day for years to come.

Have you ever had a dream where you've just won a big award or you're about to give an important presentation? You strut up to the front in front of an entire crowd and start to feel that something is off. You look down and realize you're in your underwear in front of all of these people. As they all point, laugh, and stare, the heat of your embarrassment wakes you up.

Why do people tell you to imagine others in their underwear when you're giving a speech? This can't be good advice, because you're going to spend your entire time undressing the crowd instead of focusing on your speech and what you're saying (plus that's just a little creepy).

So, why do people have these dreams of being naked in public? Well, if you're stressed, worried, concerned, or frustrated, you could feel a sense of uneasiness and feel "naked." You feel exposed to the world because your fears are making you perceive danger around you. Are you currently feeling vulnerable in your life?

During public speaking, a lot of people feel vulnerable. That's why it takes a lot of courage for some to publicly speak in front of others. In order to make an impact and create a strong bond with your audience, you need to be comfortable with yourself. You can only achieve this by feeling vulnerable.

When you're worried about an upcoming presentation or project, you may incorporate these fears into your dreams.

This nightmare can manifest from the fear you have of public speaking. You are worried about the event, so your mind is thinking of the worst possible outcomes.

Key Terms

Some of the key terms we will be discussing are listed below.

- Public speaking – Public speaking is defined as a purposeful delivery of a message from a speaker to an audience
- Channel – The channel is the category of communication taking place for the message. This can be verbal, non-verbal, or written. The channel affects how the audience will receive the message.
- Feedback – Feedback is the response from the audience to the speaker. It is their reaction to the message. Feedback can be given in the form of verbal or non-verbal cues.
- Speaker – The person who is delivering the message is the speaker.
- Audience – The group of people receiving the message.
- Noise – Noise dampens the message you're trying to send. This can be either internal or external noise. Noise can keep you from delivering your message effectively.
- Symbol – A symbol is something speakers can use to better convey their message. When you use pictures and symbols, your audience will better be able to understand what you're trying to say. Using a heart

shows love. Using a smiley face shows friendliness. Showing a red stop light means stop.

About the Book

The goals of this book are to:

1. Explain what public speaking is and why it's important
2. Discuss good and bad aspects of what makes up successful public speaking
3. Motivate you to take more public speaking opportunities
4. Give you the confidence to become a great public speaker

The book takes an overall look at what public speaking is and how to be a successful public speaker. The book is aimed at anyone who wants to be a better public speaker, especially those who have a fear of speaking in front of others.

Summarization of Chapters

In **Chapter 1** we will discuss the history and basics of public speaking. The background of public speaking is important for learning what is expected in a public speaking experience. The parts of public speaking, message, speaker, and audience are discussed in depth to explain what makes up public speaking. The chapter moves into discussing what defines a speech.

Chapter 2 focuses on the seven elements of public speaking: speaker, message, audience, channel, feedback, noise, and situation or place. The elements are broken down and then it is explained how each one plays a role in public speaking. Chapter 2 connects the elements to show the parts that go into a speech.

Chapter 3 describes the P's of performance: persuasion, passion, personal, pause, presentation, and PowerPoint. These are important aspects of public speaking and Chapter 3 does a great job of defining their impact.

In **Chapter 4**, tips and guides are shown on speech writing. Speech writing is more than just making notes. In Chapter 4 you'll find a sample outline you can use to create a speech. Using this format will help you organize your thoughts and nail your delivery.

Confidence is explained by finding your strengths and weaknesses in **Chapter 5.**

The ability to influence others is discussed in **Chapter 6**. Influencing others is a big part of public speaking. Your speech is successful when you have influenced those in your crowd. Whether that be buying a product or starting a business, your crowd will feel motivated to act when you successfully influence them.

Many people are all too familiar with stage fright. **Chapter 7** discusses what stage fright is and how it affects the body. Stage fright can hold many people back, so Chapter 7 includes tips and tricks on how to battle stage fright.

We all make mistakes. Mistakes in public speaking are common, and that's shown in **Chapter 8**. Mistakes can be avoided when you know they can happen. Being educated on the common mistakes can help you avoid trouble during your performance.

Telecommunication is today. With more and more people spending their time working from home, the amount of online presentations has exploded. Public speaking over telecommunication is a new concept, but it's broken down and discussed in **Chapter 9.**

Chapter 10 goes over public speaking and real life. The chapter includes examples of famous speeches and speakers throughout history. It discusses how to find a mentor and the importance of the venue and your clothing in public speaking.

We finish up in the **Conclusion** by summarizing the book and giving motivational advice.

Chapter One: What is Public Speaking?

You are walking down a road when you see a person standing on the side of it. They are holding a microphone and chanting with others holding signs. The one with the bullhorn is discussing oppression and wanting raises. That person is public speaking.

We've all experienced some form of public speaking, even when we aren't conscious of it. Your boss discussing next week's agenda in front of the staff is public speaking. Giving a speech at a ceremony or talking in front of a group in therapy is public speaking. Public speaking goes back to the ancient times.

The beginning of public speaking can be traced back to ancient Greece. The Greeks used public speaking mainly to persuade or praise others. Public speaking was created to increase participation from citizens in society. Public speaking was used in town gatherings and events to create a form of government and order. During these assemblies, all Greek citizens had the opportunity to oppose or suggest laws. This called for skilled public speakers. This, in turn, motivated the public to obtain public speaking skills. When Rome came to power, it adopted the Greek's public speaking methods.

After World War II, public speaking became more conversational and less formal. During the 60s and 70s, the old and new ideas of communication and public speaking were combined. This was also a time when technology really invaded the public speaking atmosphere. More people in the modern times are using computers and electronics to get their point across while giving a public speaking presentation. Even though public speaking became less formal, it comes from formal backgrounds. That's why it's so important to have a well-organized and thought-provoking public speech.

Many people want to avoid public speaking. This could be from fear or being introverted or shy. It's quite common to have a fear of public speaking, but avoiding it altogether can force you to miss out on something big.

Public speaking skills are beneficial in many areas of your life including work, school, business, and in the public arena. Public speaking is basically a live presentation in front of an audience. A speech is created when public speaking. A speech is the ability to express feelings and thoughts through speaking.

Speaking in public can include many different topics. You can talk from personal experience, academia, recreation, entertainment, and influence. Sometimes audio and visual aids can be used to better convey your message. You can use things like lights, sound, smoke, PowerPoint presentations, and songs to get your listeners' attention and keep it.

Online public speaking is different from live speaking because when you're online, people can watch at their own time. When you're speaking live, you normally have a specific time or place that it has to be done.

Public speaking is very important for businesses, because if their message is not delivered to potential customers, they cannot market their business. This means they won't be able to garner the public support to keep their business afloat.

Some of the benefits of public speaking include:
- Stronger researching skills
- Better deductive skills
- The ability to persuade others for a good cause
- Improving confidence
- Teaching yourself and others
- Positively influencing those you are speaking to
- Making a good impression
- Advancing your career
- Improving personal satisfaction
- Expanding and improving your professional network and social connections
- Increasing communication skills
- Personal development

These are just a few of the many benefits that come with public speaking. As we move through the book, you're going to learn how important public speaking is for many areas of your life.

Many colleges in the nation require a public speaking course when entering college. This is because public speaking is extremely valuable. Many students question the usefulness until they understand how it can help them in their future careers. Students can speak to professionals in their area of interest to see how often they take part in public speaking.

Some of the biggest reasons why public speaking is important are listed below.

1. Public speaking is one of the most important major communication skills that employers look for during the hiring process. Employers look for these communication skills even in entry-level positions who do not do a lot of public speaking.
    a. Nurses have presentations for first-time parents.
    b. Mangers and team-leads have meetings.
    c. Accountants present quarterly earnings to their executives.
2. Public speaking will help early students in the rest of their college career. It helps with presentation skills for future projects and requirements in class. Students enter college without expectations of how many projects and presentations they must give. Having taken the course, however, a majority of students believe that they used the information learned in public speaking often in their other classes.
3. Valuable personal benefits come with education in public speaking. Not only does public speaking improve our presentation skills, but it also improves our ability to listen

and think critically. Public speaking gives you the opportunity to take advantage of your influence and voice your concerns. It also gives you more of a control on your environment so you can face some of your fears.

4. Public speaking can change the world. Public speaking *has* changed the world, and it will continue to change it. Giving more people the knowledge of public speaking allows for more opportunities to get involved with speaking out. As more people speak out, more will participate in changes to policies, laws, culture, and leadership.

5. Strong public speaking skills can attract respect from others. When you are secure and confident in what you're saying, and how you're saying it, people will be more likely to listen to what you're saying. In turn, they will respect you more, and you'll get your message across to more people.

6. Public speaking can transform politics. Politicians are much more powerful when they are excellent public speakers. In order to win over the hearts of others, they must be able to get the crowd motivated and excited to vote for them. When we get the right people the best public speaking skills, they'll be unstoppable.

7. Public speaking expands education. Having to give a presentation shows students the importance of being prepared and being a public speaker. A teacher performs public

speaking each day in their classroom. Without public speaking, there would be no education.

8. Public speaking is communication. Communication is critical to human development and interaction. The better communication is, the better the situation is. There are many problems that can happen when communication is disrupted. Public speaking helps improve the communication of ideas, thoughts, and opinions.

The Message, the Speaker, and the Audience

The difference between public speaking and simply talking to others is the way that the information is conveyed. In public speaking, the message is created and delivered for a purpose. The focus of public speaking is simply who is saying what, to whom, using what medium, and with what effect. "Who" acts as the source of the message. "What" acts as the message itself. "Whom" is the audience receiving the message and the "medium" is the actual delivery method of the message. The "effect" is the purpose of the message. The effect is the speaker's intentions when public speaking.

Public speaking can be broken into three parts: the message, the speaker, and the audience. These three aspects make up the entire public speaking experience. Many people don't realize that they practice public speaking each day. Whether it be on a Zoom call, meeting, or giving a presentation to your boss, you're taking part in public speaking.

Public speaking doesn't have to be standing behind a podium in front of hundreds of people using a PowerPoint presentation. Being aware that you're speaking publicly can allow you to practice and give you a large advantage on your presentation. When you realize you're speaking publicly, you will be able to use your public speaking skills to improve your presentation, regardless of what type of presentation.

The message is what is being delivered to others. It includes the information, humor, details, emotional aspects, characteristics, body, and more. The message must be appropriate to the receiver (the audience). The most important parts of the message are the style, structure, and content. A strong message leads to a strong experience. The message is delivered by the speaker.

The speaker is, you guessed it, the one who is speaking to the others listening. The speaker greatly impacts the delivery and outcomes of the message. The speaker can determine motivation. If the message is powerful but the delivery is weak, the receivers will not be motivated and energized from hearing the speaker. The credibility of a speaker also goes far when delivering a message. Personality and style also influence the speaker and their ability to communicate their ideas and knowledge with the audience.

The audience is receiving the message. They are the ones who are being spoken to. This can be in various settings. The audience can be all ages, genders, populations, and more. The more a speaker can adapt to an audience, the more successful they are in delivering the message. That's why it can be important to research your audience beforehand, so you can create a better speech.

Speeches

A good speech is the foundation of public speaking. A well thought out speech can elevate your public speaking performance from mediocre to exceptional. A speech is used to deliver a specific message to your audience. Speeches can touch hearts, move nations, and create lifelong change. There are different types of speeches: entertaining, informing, demonstrative, persuasive, motivational, impromptu, oratorical, debate, and special occasion.

1. <u>An entertaining speech</u> is just what it sounds like, a speech with the intentions of entertaining others. Entertaining speeches are less formal and more about communicating emotions rather than talking with a couple facts.
    a. Entertaining speeches include toasts at weddings or an acceptance speech by an actor or artist at an award show.
2. <u>Informative speeches</u> are used to inform the audience of something. Informative speeches are meant to convey accurate information. Information is used in an informative speech to educate your audience. Typically, informative speeches have bigger, more complex ideas that are broken into smaller bite-size pieces. Informative speeches focus on statistics, facts, and studies rather than the audience's emotions.
    a. Informative speeches include those given in a meeting by staff member or a lecture from a teacher.

3. <u>Demonstrative speeches</u> seek to teach the audience how something works or how to do something. Demonstrative speeches use physical demonstration along with visual aids and information to get the message across. Many people consider informative and demonstrative speeches the same, however, informative speeches focus on "what is" and demonstrative speeches focus on "how to."

    a. Demonstrative speeches include chefs showing how to prepare a meal and a teacher writing out how to solve a math equation.

4. <u>Persuasive speeches</u> are used by the speaker to show their point of view, argue that it is right, and persuade the audience to believe and accept that point of view. Persuasive speeches can either succeed or fail. Even if you have the best speech possible for your message, if the audience isn't convinced, then it could be considered a failure. Speakers can use emotional aspects to increase persuasion as well as facts and statistics and sometimes both.

    a. A persuasive speech could be a new business idea pitch or an activist trying to spread awareness about various topics.

5. <u>A motivational speech</u> is a form of persuasive speech that aims to improve the confidence of the audience and persuade them to make changes based on your message. In a motivational speech, the speaker and the audience together set goals. The speaker gives the audience the tools they need to achieve those goals. Motivational speech focuses mainly on emotion while trying to get someone to do something.

a. A motivational speech includes a message from a football coach to the players. One of the most famous motivational speeches is the "I Have a Dream" speech by Martin Luther King Jr.

6. <u>An impromptu speech</u> is probably one of the most anxiety-provoking, public speaking situations. An impromptu speech is given without preparation or planning.

    a. Let's say you're working on a project as part of a team and your coworker all of the sudden calls out sick. Now you have to go and give an update during the executive meeting this afternoon. That's an impromptu speech.

7. <u>Oratorical speeches</u> are usually formal and pretty long.

    a. These speeches can be given during a graduation, in the attempts to address serious issues, or give comfort and mourn losses at a funeral in the form of a eulogy.

8. <u>A debate speech</u> uses figures and persuasion to justify your point of view rather than convince the audience to partake in your view such as with a persuasive speech. Debate speeches may be impromptu because you can't expect all arguments that can come from the other party until you interact with them. Once you experience a rebuttal, you have to create a debate speech to deliver on the spot supporting your stance and dismissing the opposing view. Debate speeches are very beneficial for improving public speaking skills, improving research, and developing critical thinking skills.

a. Debate speeches can be found in court trials, public forums, and legislative sessions.

9. <u>A special occasion speech</u> is an umbrella term that includes speeches that don't seem to fit in the other types. The speeches are typically short and to the point. Special occasion speeches can be impromptu, entertaining with information, and include many speeches that have various characteristics from the other types of speeches.

a. Special occasion speeches are for weddings, office parties, birthdays, introductions, and much more.

Speeches have various characteristics that can be used when classifying. Many speeches will include characteristics from more than one type of speech. But the type of speech is determined from its goal.

For example, if you're using information to entertain others, it is an entertainment speech. If you are using humor and entertainment to persuade others, then it is a persuasion speech. Although the speeches have various characteristics the goal of the speech determines the type of the speech. Once you have the goal of your speech, you can determine the type of speech you need.

Public speaking is fully made up of seven elements:
1. Speaker
2. Message
3. Audience
4. Channel
5. Feedback

6. Noise

7. Place

The seven elements of public speaking are important for crafting your public speaking presentation. You'll learn how to be a great speaker, how to craft a strong message, create a connection with the audience, optimize your channel, use feedback, prepare for noise, and pick your place of presentation.

Chapter Two: 7 Elements of Public Speaking

For an effective presentation or speech in public, the speaker has to prepare and transmit seven elements. Ignoring these staples during presenting can lead to a bad outcome. The seven elements are the speaker, the message, the audience, the channel, feedback, noise, and the place.

When you're planning a presentation, use the seven elements as a guide to build your speech. If you build your presentation around these seven elements, it will create a strong message – regardless of the topic. You can count on these elements to bring out your best side.

If you set down to start a speech and don't know where to start, look to these elements. They will guide you through creating the perfect message. First, you have to start with yourself.

Element 1: The Speaker

The speaker is one of the most important parts of public speaking (obviously). The speaker is the source of the message. No matter how many visual aids you use or how good they are, it will still boil down to the speaker to deliver the message appropriately. Visual aids are a great addition to presentation, but it's important not to rely on them 100%. If there were to be an issue delivering the visual aids, your entire performance could crumble without a good speaker. Three of the most important aspects of the speaker are motivation, credibility, and style and personality.

Motivation

To give a good performance, a speaker must be motivated to give a good performance. If you're not motivated, even the simplest of tasks can be so hard. Lack of motivation can create many problems for us. It can keep us from doing and enjoying the things we love the most. A lack of motivation can be a sign of stress or depression. If you feel stressed about public speaking, you are less likely to be motivated to public speak. If you're not motivated when you speak, you could give a mediocre performance.

If you're not motivated for your speech, then you're not going to work hard for it. You're going to do just what needs to be done to get it over with, instead of getting it done while exceeding expectations. Exceeding expectations is a great way to impress others. It's easier to impress others when you're motivated while speaking.

Being motivated shows passion. When you're motivated to speak, you're going to care more about your performance. When you're motivated to speak it seems obvious that you're passionate about your outcome. Speaking with motivation means you're speaking with a purpose. Your words are purposeful and include valuable information instead of just filler sentences. If you show your passion, you can get your message across more clearly.

When you're speaking with motivation, you're also more likely to smile, be open, move around more, and be more animated. This isn't just fun for you, but it's also fun for your audience. They get to watch you move around and basically act out your presentation while they use your visual aids and listen to your voice to catch all aspects of the message. When you and your audience are both having a good time, you leave a good impression on them.

Now, we all know motivation cannot come with the snap of a finger. If it were that easy, everybody would be constantly motivated to go to the gym. Motivation comes from inside, but it can be built from the outside. In order to get more motivated for an upcoming public speaking project, research more about your topic. You're likely to find something interesting or something you haven't heard before, and it can make you excited to proceed with the project. You can go and tell others your new knowledge.

You can ask around for more about your topic. You can speak to people with experience in what you're talking about and even gather a few stories that you could use during your presentation. This can create a stronger bond between you and your topic and therefore increase your motivation to speak about it. It can also give you a better idea of your topic so it's easier to talk about.

Rewards and incentives can also be used for motivation. What positives are you getting from this? Are you enjoying the ability to teach others? Are you getting some sort of award or winning a competition with this project? Focusing on the good that can come from your speech can improve your desire to public speak.

Take advantage of the opportunity to public speak. You can create new friends or network connections. You could create new opportunities for yourself. You could be proud of yourself when you're done speaking. This is an opportunity to show others, and yourself, what you're worth. It's the perfect opportunity to show what you can do. You can learn more about your topic and public speaking.

Credibility

There are three stages of credibility: initial, derived, and terminal. Initial credibility is the audience's opinion, or what they know, before the speech. Derived credibility is the perceptions of the audience during the speech. Terminal credibility means what the audience thinks when leaving the speech. You're going to want to build credibility before, during, and after the speech to deliver a longer lasting impact on the audience, as well as an increase in trust.

When you're building initial credibility, you need to understand if the audience thinks you're trustworthy and what they know about your expertise. Do they know you professionally or personally? This can affect the way the audience sees you throughout the speech. You are going to want to consider initial credibility as your own personal branding. It's what makes up who you are and what the audience knows about you. If your reputation precedes you, then you know your audience may know you pretty well. That doesn't mean everyone will, and so you may have to rely on the introduction given before the speech.

During an introduction, a moderator or host will give relevant information about you and your background. This will build your initial credibility. If your reputation precedes you then it will add to your initial credibility. So, an introduction is a great way to start off your speech. There is not always going to be a host or moderator to introduce you. It's important to learn how to introduce yourself to improve your initial credibility.

If your crowd doesn't know you beforehand, the introduction is going to be their very first time seeing and hearing about you. The more you can teach the crowd about yourself the better your relationship will form. The better relationship between you and your audience leads to them being better listeners. Your introduction can determine the audience's reaction throughout the speech. A good introduction prepares your audience for the rest of your speech and can build a strong foundation for an impressive speech.

<u>Tips for a Solid Introduction</u>

1. Capture the attention of your audience. It's helpful to use a short, attention-grabbing statement. Some good options for an attention grabber are an interesting story, a relevant quote, a thought-provoking question, or interesting statistics or facts. It's best to pick something that's going to fit your presentation the best and remember not to overthink it.

2. Welcome your audience to your presentation. A genuine, quick welcome can make the audience feel appreciated. It can help them listen better, but if it's too long, then you create

a risk of losing the audience's interest. You can also thank them for coming to hear you speak.

3. Introduce yourself. A brief, thoughtful introduction can create a memorable and powerful feeling throughout the audience. If you make your introduction too long, the audience are going to feel like they're getting your life story. You can disclose any relevant or interesting information that will help your initial credibility.

4. Give your purpose as to why you're speaking. The purpose of the presentation is one of the critical parts of the introduction. A lot of times your audience is already going to be familiar with your topic, but it's a good way to make sure everyone is clear and on the same page. Be specific when talking about your purpose by stating the goal of your presentation.

5. Discuss how you're going to be taking questions. Some speakers take questions at the end of the presentation. Others take them throughout the presentation and just want people to raise their hands. There are even some speakers that want the audience to just yell out their questions when they get them. Make sure you tell the audience how you handle questions, and that way it doesn't throw you off throughout the presentation or confuse others.

6. Go over any additional details that the audience might need to know. It could be extra information on yourself or the material you're

going over. You can cover any handouts or invites that will be given to the audience. That way the audience can focus on you instead of the handouts or the items they may be given.

7. Don't overdo the introduction or the thank you. You don't want your audience to be exhausted before the speech actually starts. Keep it short and brief in the beginning and you can re-clarify at the end.

When an introduction is too long, you lose the interest of the audience. The faster you can get to the material that they are happy about hearing, the better. A well-planned introduction will only be between 5 to 10 minutes. Anything longer and you risk losing the momentum from the introduction.

Derived credibility is how the audience looks at you during the speech. It includes their perception of you and the material you're delivering. Derived credibility is established based on how the audience reacts to the words you use, the delivery, what you're wearing, and the way you carry yourself during the presentation. You can increase your perceived competence by using strong facts and supporting evidence while explaining it to the audience. If your communication with the audience is sincere and honest, you're going to improve your character perception.

Derived credibility comes from everything the speaker is saying and doing during the speech. Even if you have a great initial credibility, if you can't follow through to positive derived credibility, then it could affect your entire speech.

Think about your favorite pop star before they come on stage. Their initial credibility is high because they are famous for being a good singer. But if they get on stage and you realize they are lip-syncing, it is going to negatively affect their derived credibility.

You can increase your derived credibility with the audience by using strong, confident, and assertive styles and language. If you show a genuine concern for the audience, you're going to increase your credibility. You can show concern for your audience by asking them questions. Establishing common ground with your audience can improve their positive perceptions of you. In order to establish a common ground, you can disclose parts of your background and experience that are similar to those in the audience. When you create this connection, the audience is more likely to feel like they know you and you know them, which improves trust.

Connect with your audience by using examples they can understand. Relevant examples are important for allowing the audience to use the material that they're learning in real life scenarios. They can take the new information that they are learning and connect it with their previous experience by using an example. This increases the audiences grasp of the material. Using these examples can also allow you to be more comfortable speaking because your audience understands better.

Think of some real-life scenarios that you have experienced that are similar to what you're speaking on. If you did more research into your project, now is the time that you can use the dialogue that you gained from speaking with those experienced in your topic. You have their personal experience and the material to make an understandable example for your audience.

<u>Terminal credibility</u> can be created based upon the rapport built with the audience. You want your terminal credibility to be better than your initial credibility. If you want to leave a long lasting and good impression, this can be done with positive terminal credibility. Rapport is when two or more people perceive being in-sync, or on the same brain wavelengths, because of similarities and relations with others. People can create positive rapport when they relate to each other. Creating a rapport with your audience means relating to them.

When you have such a good terminal credibility, it can carryover past the speech. Your terminal credibility could become your initial credibility. With good terminal credibility comes a preceding reputation. Be aware though that not all proceeding reputations are positive. Lasting impression you leave on your audience could be stronger than your initial presence.

Terminal credibility can improve from derived credibility. For example, you may express views and experiences of yourself that your audience can relate to. If you disclose your favorite sports team and your audience members feel the same way about that team, they are going to view you more positively. When it comes to understanding if your audience trusts you, it's more about the attitude the listeners have in their mind. It's not so much about the source or characteristics of the speaker. People will decide on their own if they trust you. You just have to give them reasons to show that you are trustworthy. If your audience trusts you, they're going to listen to you more and improve your terminal credibility.

The conclusion of your speech or presentation is the time when audience members start to begin their terminal credibility beliefs. Once the audience understands that you've reached the conclusion, they know the presentation is about to be over. They begin collecting their thoughts on you, the material, and the presentation. The conclusion is a good time to thank your audience again and show your appreciation for them for being a part of your presentation. When the listeners feel appreciated, they have better chances of improving your terminal credibility.

Your terminal credibility can determine what the audience is going to do with the material next. If they trust you and they think you're credible, they may take your material and run with it. If they don't think you're credible, they may dismiss everything that you said. Overall, credibility is about the attitude of the audience instead of any specific trait of the speaker. At the end, the audience is going to decide based on evidence and knowledge about you what your credibility is. Not everyone is going to agree on your credibility, so it's important to approach everyone cautiously. You cannot assume the entire audience feels one way just because a few do.

Hey, the audience is going to remember your goodwill. They want to know if this speaker has positive ethical intentions toward the listeners. If your listeners perceive you as an ethical speaker, they are more likely to deem you credible.

Initial credibility can affect derived credibility. Derived credibility can affect terminal credibility. Once someone has made up their mind about you, they may tune out everything else you say. That is why it is so important to understand the three parts of credibility so that way you create a better credibility with your audience even if it's after the speech. Credibility can generally determine if the audience is going to trust and believe what you say or not. Do you want them to believe you? Then you need to give them a reason to.

Overall, in order to improve your credibility, you are going to want to focus on your initial credibility, derived credibility, and terminal credibility. When you combine these three types of credibility, you're sure to gain the audience's trust. You want to use your initial, derived, and terminal credibility to establish a positive overall credibility.

Style and Personality

An audience wants a speaker who can positively communicate their knowledge and ideas. An audience wants a relatable and refreshing style, personality, and speaker. A speaker's style is the individual way that information is given to the audience. In order to improve communication, the speaker's style must relate to the speeches content.

- If your objective is to motivate your crowd, you want to use an upbeat and exciting style. Use lots of room on stage and wide arm movements. Move around and use big facial expressions. You can say things to the crowd and make them repeat it back. You can ask them questions and have them raise their hands.

- If your objective is to persuade your audience, you might want to use exciting and loud running-around-the-stage behavior. You can use hand movements and gestures when speaking to keep the attention of your crowd, but not overwhelm them while you're giving critical information.

- If you're giving a serious or formal presentation, you may want to use a slower pace and keep your hand gestures under control. You can give minimal humor but enough engaging material so the audience feels a connection.

A speaker can have many different styles. A good speaker is able to read their audience and change their style as needed. Being a fluid presenter allows you to keep a constant emotional attachment with the audience. The style of speaking goes farther than just your actions, however. Your style also includes what you're saying and how you're saying it. You could have a content-rich style.

A content-rich style means the speaker presents facts that are important to the audience. Content-rich speakers stick to the important, objective information. These types of speakers can be beneficial for those who want to get a lot of information in a timely way. A funny speaker uses jokes and excitement to entertain the audience. A comedian can be a funny speaker.

Some speakers are also storytellers. They use a long story about their life. Then they go back and connect parts of their life to what they learned. An example of this would be a TED Talk. You may have a speaker who is talking about how they reached success. They may discuss a pivotal moment in their life such as a large success or a large failure. Storytellers aim to use a story as a building block for their speech and their message. A storyteller relates with the audience but doesn't necessarily use factual information.

Personality also plays a large role in public speaking. The audience can see when you're being genuine. When you're being genuine you seem more trustworthy. When you're being genuine you are creating authentic moments where you can speak from the heart. The audience can see these authentic moments and that's when the connection grows. Even if you are a little weird it could let the audience to see the real you and make a real connection.

You will never need to change your personality. You are just going to find your powers, strengths, and the skills that you already have to adapt to the presentation. Everyone has their own strengths. You exploit the powerful aspects of your personality to create the connection. You can adapt your style, but never your personality.

Don't be egotistical and try to manipulate your audience. They will sense that you're fake and stop listening and respecting you. Don't be pushy or too aggressive or your audience will feel threatened or offended. Don't try to use mind tricks and some hypnosis psychology that you found online. You're going to get better credibility when your true personality shines through.

Element 2: The Message

The message is everything the speaker says, bodily and verbally. The verbal component of the message includes content and structure. The content is what is being said about the topic or subject. The style is the way the content of the speech is delivered. The structure of a message is determined by its organization.

Content can be guided with a few tips:

- Use an attention-getting device
- Tell stories or examples throughout that relate to your topic
- Know the purpose and goal of your speech
- Include new information in the speech
- Use an internal and ending summary
- Create a memorable exit line

Content in public speaking is what the speaker is talking about. The topic of the conversation is going to be the main idea of what the speaker talks about. Content can be created from facts, history, experience, academia, and much more. One of the most important pieces of content from any speech is the main goal of the presentation. This thesis statement is going to determine what your content is made up of. Think of if you had to put your entire speech into one sentence. If you completely condensed your speech into one sentence, what would it be? That is your thesis statement.

Content should also be refreshing. Refreshing meaning that it is a new piece of information. Now, your information may be new for a lot of your audience, and there are some that may already be educated on the topic. In this case you need to try to find some information that they don't know. This could be from an interview, an uncommon source of information, or a recent event. Do you want your audience to be intrigued by your content? You want your content to stick out in the minds of your audience.

Strong content means it is relevant to the audience and your topic. If your topic is IT management and you spend most of your time talking about something that is not related, then your content is going to be irrelevant and won't be remembered by the listeners. Regardless of the speaker, the content must match what the speech is going to be about.

Strong content also has a summary. In your speech, you could have an internal summary. An internal summary can be located in the middle of the speech to show the progress you are making towards the end of your speech. This can be a recap of what you have gone over and a refresher for the new information you are about to cover. This recap and summary improve the organization of your content.

Organization is critical for delivering an effective message. If your facts are all over the place, and nothing seems to be in order, then your audience is going to get lost trying to keep up with you. They are going to be more focused on trying to decipher what you are saying instead of hearing what you are saying. Organization can keep the audience from being confused, and it can ease them into the topic you will be discussing. For example, you may want to start off your speech with some of the basic principles and ideas of what you'll be discussing. It can set up a foundation for the rest of the content in the speech.

The exit line is one of the most important parts of the speech because it leaves an impression on the audience. The exit line could be a quote or a last bit of outstanding advice. This will resonate with your crowd. People will best remember what you said last.

The structure of a message is important for the delivery. You're going to want to spend the majority of time and attention on the body of your message. The introduction and conclusion should make up about 10% each, leaving 80% for the body. You can structure your material in many ways.

- A chronological structure is the arrangement of material on a timeline. You have the beginning, middle, and end. This would be a presentation that includes events throughout history. You could be talking about the history of the country or your company.

- Non-chronological structure can also talk about events, but not necessarily in order. You can use multiple events from multiple times to connect them to various ideas. In this case, they don't have to be in order.

- An even, balanced structure means having the information stretched out appropriately. If you spend 60% of your time talking about a microdetail, then you won't have time to cover the other important parts of the speech- or you will have to rush through them, which leaves the audience rushing to write notes or completely missing the point altogether.

- A powerful-flow structure is the flow of information that gains intensity as you move through your presentation. You could start with a small fire and lead into a forest fire. You can start with some believable and common facts while leading to some astounding material.

- A climactic structure keeps your audience's attention throughout your delivery. You can keep them attached with the question to an answer but delivering the answer at the end. This main question (such as, "How to make $100,000 a year as a realtor") could be answered throughout the speech, then ending with the final answer at the end (buy older homes, flip them, then sell).

- The melodrama structure is where a speaker uses a personal story, in the same sense of structure as a movie. You meet the speaker and see their circumstances. Then there's normally a tragedy that leads to the author being triumphant over the problem. A melodrama structure engages the audience through an emotional journey (this will also improve credibility).

- The tower structure is about using the different layers of information that grabs the attention of the audience and supports your key message. When you and your audience finish building the structure, you can both look at the power of what you've built.

- A mystery structure means using a question or problem to structure your message. Your audience can be desperate for the answer or solution so they will set on the edge of their seats and listen until they get the answer.

- The ping pong structure is an argumentative speech that goes "back and forth" between opposing sides. This structure is beneficial for an unbiased presentation of a topic. If someone is trying to give a neutral explanation of two sides of an argument, a ping pong structure may be the best bet.

Regardless of the structure, you are going to want to arrange your material in a way that motivates your listener to act on your words. No matter the reason of your presentation, you want others to feel comfortable taking your work and using it in their lives.

The structure should be based on the speaker, the message, and the audience. The speaker can create the structure of the speech so they understand it so clearly that they can teach others. If the content of the message is complex, you may want to arrange the information in a way that keeps simple information first and then moves onto the more complex ideas. This gives the audience a chance to digest the basic principles and use them to build the off of the new information.

The structure should be focused on the most important parts of your speech. The longer your presentation, the more likely the audience is going to feel overwhelmed. You don't want to dump a large part of your information on your audience all at once then ask them to remember it all. Create your structure in a way that makes sure the audience is going to remember the most important parts.

Studies show that people are more likely to remember the beginning and ending of something, rather than what's in the middle. The middle can get lost in the noise and become diluted with other information. Structure your most important information around the beginning and end.

This is why it's important to include a thesis and conclusion. Typically, you can hold someone's attention for seven minutes before they drift off into thinking of other stuff. Deliver some of your most important information at the beginning, such as a summarization of your speech and what you're going to go over. You can let the audience know what you're going to be talking about and what you're trying to gain from public speaking.

Organization in a structure is critical for delivery. Organization keeps your information straight, so you don't have to make rash decisions while presenting. When you organize your thoughts, you are more prepared for what may go wrong, or different, and handle it more appropriately. Organization also gives your audience a "road map" while listening to the message. When they can see you are clearly organized, they find it easier to concentrate and follow along.

Structure can also help if you have to shave down your speech. If you jot down all of your ideas and collect all the information you want to tell, it could become overwhelming. You want to create your speech, then structure it in a way that the extra bits of unnecessary information are shaved off. Even if these are your favorite parts of the speech, if the content doesn't support the structure, then it should be taken out. This way your audience gets what they want, when they want, and how they want.

Use a structure that matches the complexity of your content. If you use an over-simplified structure, it can make your content look weak. If you use too strong of a structure around weak content, it can make you seem uptight. Once you find the perfect structure for your content, you can focus on the next element.

Element 3: The Audience

An audience analysis is created when you know who you are going to be speaking in front of. You may get a general idea of your audience based on the topic you're discussing. It is safe to say that those who are listening to you either have an interest in the topic or have experience with your content. You can use this to create advantages in your speech.

It's important to create a relationship with your audience when public speaking. You can create a stronger relationship with them when you research about them beforehand. No matter how big or small your presentation is going to be, researching your audience can benefit the outcomes of your speech.

What to Look for When Doing Audience Research

After you pick out your public speaking topic, it is time to research your audience. You know what you're going to say, so now you have to learn *how* to say it. It is beneficial if you research your audience before you create your speech, so you will know how to structure it. You know what you need to use and what you need to avoid before you start writing. This way you don't waste time by having to go back and change parts of your speech. More than likely, your speech will change many times. You can save time on these changes by making plans around your audience. Consider including the following research:

- *Interests.* You want to learn more about what they like. When you see what they like, you can include more of that in your speech. If you find out what they don't like, then you know what to avoid when creating your presentation. You may also find similarities in your likes, so you can use this to create a bond.

- *Age.* When you're speaking to a younger audience, you may want to use a casual, up-beat tone with slang and in an informal manner. You will be able to better connect with your younger audience when discussing recent events and how they can be related to what you're talking about. If you're talking to an older audience, you may want to use more traditional language and presentation tactics. Once you know their age, you can make a more age-appropriate speech.

- *Education level.* Some of your audience may be experts in the field, while others are just making contact with this information. You will not want to keep your entire speech in the basic level because it will lose the interest of those who are experts. Just the same, you don't want to keep the content in an expert area for the entire time because it will annoy and discourage those who are just learning.

- *Attitudes.* It's important to know the attitudes of your audience so you don't create any trouble during your speech. If you say something that is blatantly against the attitudes of your listeners, they may get up and leave or try to start trouble. Understanding the attitudes of your audience keeps you from crossing the line between informative to insulting.

- *Beliefs.* You can focus on religion if you're looking to understand the beliefs of your audience. Knowing what your audience believes can help you better create a speech because you can choose the proper content material.

Doing some research on your audience pays off when you're creating your speech. When you want to impress your audience, tailor your performance around them. Doing research on your audience will give you information on them. You can use this information to include certain parts of information in your content. There are many benefits that come with doing some research on your audience.

- You know what language to use. When you're writing about a topic, do you use formal or informal language? The characteristics of your audience will help you determine what kind of language will be best used.
  - Language should be vivid, inclusive, appropriate, and familiar. Appropriate language means understanding the difference of negative and positive language. Appropriate language means the language is fitting to the audience, the setting, the speech, and for ourselves.
  - An example of negative language would be using curse words or inappropriate words in a

delicate setting. If you are public speaking at a church, for example, there are certain words and phrases that you want to avoid. An example of positive language would be using master terms when dealing with an audience that is experienced in your topic.

- You have a better idea of your audience's energy. If you are dealing with older people, the style may be quieter and more formal. If you are dealing with younger people, the style can be more casual with higher energy. If you are public speaking at a prison, morale might be low. Once you have a better idea of the audience's energy when coming into a public speaking event you can better guess the outcomes. Matching your energy to the audiences will help you with message execution.

- It is easier to make a connection with your audience. Sometimes the audience already knows the public speaker before the show starts because of an advertisement pamphlet with hosts listed. When the speaker takes the time to learn the audience, they can create a relationship during the public speaking event.

Element 4: The Channel

The channel is the speaker's use of non-verbal and verbal communication. The channel defines the way the speaker delivers the message. When face-to-face, the speaker uses audio (sounds from their words) to translate the message to the audience. The speaker can also use facial expressions, hand movements and gestures, and project images and words on a screen to deliver their message as well. These are all channels.

When you're delivering a speech over a computer, the computer would be the channel. If you're using music in your speech, or pictures on a screen, these would all be channels. Channels include any way that the speaker can get the message to the audience. The audience captures the message through their audio (hearing) and visual (sight) channels. Most speeches will take place using audio and visual channels.

Some non-verbal channels include:

- Gestures
- Facial expression
- Movement
- Posture
- Body language

Visual channels can include:

- Drawings
- Diagrams
- Photographs
- Graphics
- Objects
- Videos

Auditory channels are:

- Voice volume
- Tone
- CDS, audio materials, and tapes

Element 5: Feedback

To maximize your potential to be a great public speaker, you need feedback to determine how well you're doing.

- Feedback is information received from your audience about your performance in a presentation or speech. It can be interpreted and used to show how good (or bad) you're doing. It can be brief or extensive. It can also come in multiple forms.
- Useful feedback is feedback you get that can help you improve your speaking skills. This can be through delivery, writing, visual design, or more.
- Useless feedback is just that- useless. For example, if your audience answers a questionnaire after the presentation and they say that the room was too cold and the food was bad, that isn't much advice or insight for you to use to become a better public speaker.
- Positive feedback reinforces something you've done or said.
- Negative feedback goes against what you've been saying or suggests that the audience was unhappy with the presentation or the speaker.
- Verbal feedback means that during the speech you can get feedback from your audience by asking a question and getting a verbal response.

- Non-verbal feedback is any type of feedback you receive that's not verbal. When you're in front of your audience, non-verbal behavior can be an important cue to see what the audience understands. It can also show the attention level, agreement or excitement, or disagreement or confusion.

- An Audience Response System is also a really fascinating non-verbal feedback device. For example, on *Who Wants to be a Millionaire*, when the contestant uses the "audience for help" line, the audience can respond to a question through a tablet or wireless keypad. Then the results are displayed on a screen.
  - As a public speaker looking for audience feedback, you can ask a question and have the audience respond to you via text, smartphone, tablet, etc.

Feedback is a vital element to look for when public speaking. Feedback consists of the process where the speaker receives a response or information from the audience that heard the message. The feedback process is completed when the speaker responds to the feedback. It's important for speakers to respond to feedback because it shows the audience that the speaker is paying attention to them.

Speaking in public means you have to pay attention to the non-verbal reactions of your listeners. This means you should be prepared to respond to these reactions during your presentation. This goes back to adapting your tone, style, and speech to your audiences. If your audience looks bored, you can transfer to some more high energy movements and information. If your audience looks interested, you can be sure to speak loudly and utilize your most important information at this time.

Feedback means being able to read your audience. Sometimes you may not be able to read them, or you're collecting information that isn't very useful. Some feedback is uncomfortable to receive. The audience can show their feedback through verbal and non-verbal channels. They can vibe off of your energy. If you are nervous and scared, it can make them cautious and uninterested. If you are high energy and moving a lot, your audience can be interested and engaged.

Feedback can be verbal or non-verbal. Verbal feedback can be given when the audience asks a question or gets your attention when they don't understand. Some listeners may also speak out when they agree or disagree to something. When you hear verbal feedback, be sure to acknowledge and address it.

Non-verbal feedback can be expressed by the audience through agreement or excitement, their level of attentiveness, disagreement, confusion, and quality of understanding. Non-verbal feedback does not have to be silent. It can be a grunt of disagreement or approval, clapping, or other intentional vocalizations. However, more often non-verbal feedback is body language that is done either consciously or subconsciously by the audience.

There are many ways in which you can watch your audience for feedback that you may not be able to hear. If you pay attention, though, you can almost always see the feelings of your audience. Some things to look for include:

    1. Boredom. Boredom can be shown through someone tilting their head to one side. Or if you can see that they're looking right at you,

but they're not focused, their minds could be elsewhere.

2. Eye contact. If you audience isn't making eye contact with you, then they may not be listening. Although this isn't always true, it's important to have your audience looking at you as much as possible. Their eyes may look around or stay consistent with yours. If someone is fiddling with something, but they are looking at you, there could be a chance they are distracted. You know you have their attention if they are making eye contact and they are genuinely listening.

3. Disbelief. Disbelief can be shown in listeners by touching the ear, scratching the chin, or averting their gaze. If someone in your audience isn't convinced by what you're saying, they could be confused.

4. Body posture and position. It is common for the audience to mostly face the speaker when intently listening. If your audience isn't engaged, they may turn themselves away from the speaker.

5. Leaving the room. If lots of people keep entering and leaving the room, chances are you don't have the audience's attention or interest enough to keep them in the room.

You're going to notice things about your audience while you are giving your presentation. They may distract you with the things they are doing. If you get distracted and focus on how they aren't paying attention, it can throw you off of where you are in your speech. It's important to collect yourself and try to calmly make a decision if you notice that your audience is confused or not engaged. If you think you are losing your audience then chances may be that you actually are.

If you notice your audience's eyes are wandering, you can bring them back to focus with a question. The question can be anything you can think of in the moment. It can be about something you're currently speaking about, their opinion on what you're saying, or if they are confused about anything. You can just stop and ask, "is everyone on the same page?" or, "is everyone following?" You could even bring attention to it in a humorous way. You can say, "Look, guys, I know we are all tired from lunch," or, "the dreary weather is dragging us all down."

Other than asking a question, you could also physically engage your audience. If you notice you aren't connecting with your audience, have them connect with each other. If you are in the middle of speaking about a subject and you notice your audience is bored, you can take a moment to have your audience speak to each other. You can say, "Pick a person near you and tell them what you're thinking right now about the subject," or, "ask your neighbor what they would do if. . ."

Bringing your audience's attention to themselves allows their minds to return to the room and therefore back to you. On average we can hold someone's attention for seven minutes before it drips away to something else. It happens to everyone. It's just important to recognize when this is happening for the majority of the room and learn how to bring them back.

In some circumstances of feedback, you can be better prepared to take the criticism. For example, after a presentation if the audience is asked to give their views on speaker via questionnaire. In this instance, you have the ability to mentally prepare for what you're about to read. There are some situations, however, where you cannot prepare to receive negative feedback. In the situation it's important to understand how to control yourself and approach the negative feedback appropriately.

Let's say you may be giving a presentation on a current political event. It is well known that politics can create many conflicting beliefs. Being in politics is a sensitive world even without offending or disagreeing with someone else. Because of that, it's likely that one of your audience members may speak out against what you were saying or presenting. Many times, this is unpredictable, so you must be on your toes with your listeners.

If you have received unexpected negative feedback, it is important to remember a few things:

1. This speaking presentation does not define who you are as a public speaker. You, as a whole public speaker, are made up of all of your public speaking experiences. This one experience will not make or break who you are. So, don't be discouraged if you get this negative feedback.

2. Stay calm and see it as an opportunity. If you are receiving negative feedback, they are telling you what they did not like about you or the presentation. This gives you an inside opportunity to change certain

aspects about your presentation in order to be better for next time.

3. Try not to get upset, especially angry. Becoming angry can ruin the presentation and possibly destroy any relationships you had created with the audience. You have to understand that everybody is different and everyone in the room may feel differently about you. This may have nothing to do with who you are as a public speaker and more about what they believe. We all have the ability and freedom to believe what we want, so be respectful of their views as long as you are respectful of theirs.

4. Take control of the situation. If one of your audience members is making a scene because of something they believe is conflicting, you may want to resort to security if the situation cannot get under control. It's important to understand your security and resources before your speech starts.

    a. In this situation you can try to answer the question broadly or let them know that you have heard them, and now it is time to move on with the presentation. You can say something along the lines of, "I hear what you're saying, and thank you for sharing that, so now we're going to move onto the next part."

    b. You can also create answers that may defuse the situation. You may say things like, "I'm not sure, but I will look more into it," or, "that's a great question/point. We may talk more about that later."

c. You can also offer to meet them one on one after the presentation. You can say, "Why don't we move on with the presentation and open up for questions at the end?"

Element 6: Noise

Noise can prevent the audience from hearing you. No matter how hard the speaker tries, no message is ever received the way that the sender intends because of the constant noise that exists in communication. Noise is found in all parts of communication. Noise can be considered both internal and external.

Noise can be unpleasant and affect the morale in the room. If there is construction going on outside of your office, it can irritate you and your listeners. If there are other people giving presentations in the rooms around, that can distract you and your crowd. Therefore, noise can affect the receiving and sending of your message.

External noise refers to a noisy room or your physical environment and your physiological state. Think of giving an outdoor speech near a busy freeway or in front of many talkative teenagers. Psychological and semantic noise are referred to as internal noise. Internal noise can prevent you from delivering your message effectively. Noise is unavoidable no matter if it's external or internal. There are tips and tricks you can take, however, to decrease as much noise as possible.

In order to fight external noise, you can see if you have a microphone or sound system that can be used. You can also just speak louder or determine if the noise can be lowered or stopped. If it's the people that are being loud, you can simply do something to get their attention such as clap or start a song or turn on your presentation slides.

In order to fight internal noise before speaking, you can take some deep breaths. You're going to want to exhale all of the negative anxiety and self-doubt you have regarding your presentation. Inhale the confidence. After all, internal noise can come from stress, nervousness, or anxiety. These deep breaths should shut down your internal monologue and let you start building yourself up.

Sometimes we can hear noise and sometimes we can't. If everyone was able to perfectly get the message across there would never be conflict and never be any creativity. Noise can come from both the speaker and listener. There also may be noise that isn't related to the speaker or the listener. There are four types of noise: physical, physiological, psychological, and semantic.

Physical noise is any external noise that interferes with the speaker and the listener. This physical noise harms the physical transfer of the message or signal. Some physical noises are loud kids, air conditioners, the hum of electronics, neighbors, and more.

Physiological noise is started by barriers between the receiver and the sender. Some examples of physiological noise are:

- Articulation
- Talking too fast or too slow
- Forgetting to pause or breathe

- Slurring of words
- Talking too quiet

One type of physiological noise that comes from the listener is hearing problems. The difficulty to hear the words, whether it be due to low or high tone, can be considered physiological noise.

Psychological noise is the mental interference in the listener or speaker. Some types of psychological noises include sarcasm, previous knowledge, a wandering mind, ignorance, and more. A wandering mind is mainly a problem associated with being a listener. If your listener gets distracted, they can have a problem keeping up with you. This can lead to confusion or inability to discuss new ideas.

If we aren't talking appropriately or at a good speed, the speaker can cause a listener to get a wandering mind. If they can't keep up or are confused about what you're saying, they'll start to think about other things. Wandering thoughts are a problem for the speaker as well.

If you see something in the crowd that distracts you, you may lose your train of thought. You also may start talking about one thing and move onto another, then get side-tracked with your new story. It takes concentration to stay on track when you're being affected by noise.

Previous education can create psychological noise in many ways. When someone believes they already know something, it can be hard for them to listen to someone else. Psychological noise includes:

- Preconceived ideas
- Biases
- Presuppositions
- Closed-mindedness
- Prejudices

When you encounter people who have these mindsets, it can be harder to get them to listen to new perspectives. People with these mindsets tend to bring them into the room with them. It can be hard to get people to listen to you if they already have ideas about what you're talking about. Now, not only do you have to give your presentation, but you also have to convince them to listen.

If your listener doesn't agree with you, you can always use sarcasm. However, sarcasm is a type of psychological noise. If your audience doesn't agree with what you're saying, then sarcasm will ensure that they don't pay attention to your presentation. If you give sarcasm, it can disrupt your crowd. Once they reply back with their reaction, it's going to be noise to you. Once you are sending noise back-and-forth, true communication will stop.

Semantic noise is when the listener and the speaker have different meaning systems. It can cause confusion when one word has a different definition between the speaker and the audience. Jargon and slang can be semantic noise. Jargon can make communication quick and clear when everyone agrees to the meaning of a word. Jargon can become noise when listeners have different ideas of the word. This can get really noisy for people who are not involved in your current field.

Semantic noise includes sentences and words that are ambiguous. It can be very hard for some people to speak concretely. The speaker can create semantic noise if they use too many abstract words and ideas. If your audience thinks that your words are too abstract, then it creates semantic noise.

No matter the type or place, in communication you will never be able to completely get rid of noise for every person in your audience. There are ways, however, that you can reduce the noise for your audience as well as yourself.

1. Make sure to use precise language. Make sure that your listeners will be able to understand your words. This can reduce semantic noise.
2. Practice as much as you can. Practice so that way you can avoid noise when you come in to contact with it or keep it from bothering you and your audience. The more you practice the more you are going to be able to determine what noise is taking away from the clarity of your message. Not only will you be able to handle the noise as it shows itself, but you will also be able to take steps to prevent noise.
3. Ask others for their feedback. Invite feedback often so you can know the types of noise that your audience encountered. This way you can better prepare for next time. We can also learn more about what you did to cause noise.

Element 7: Situation or Place

The situation is the time and place that the conversation happens. The situation is the physical setting of where the event is taking place. There are three speaking situations we may find ourselves in: interactive, non-interactive, and partially interactive.

In interactive speaking situations, both parties can talk and interact such as in phone calls and face-to-face conversations. Both the speaker and the listener switch roles. In this situation, both parties can be speakers and listeners at the same time. The roles interchange and move with the conversation. Each person can ask for something to be repeated, clarified, expanded on, and more.

In partially interactive speaking situations, the idea is that the audience doesn't generally interrupt the speech. This would be like delivering a speech to an audience. This may be the majority of where public speaking presentations span from. In these situations, the speaker can use non-verbal cues to gather enough feedback from the audience to alter the presentation.

In non-interactive speaking situations, the speech is typically recorded and there is no interaction at all. This would be like recording a lecture and posting it to YouTube or to a work website. Even in non-interactive speaking situations, however, you may still have to look for noise.

When you step back and look at the seven elements, it can seem overwhelming. However, once you learn techniques on how to improve these elements, it's going to become second nature. It's not that you have to memorize each step.

Just learn the ways you can use the elements in your presentation. Experiment and test different ways to utilize the most of these elements. You're going to find practices that best suit you, your audience, and your presentation.

Chapter Three: The P's of Performance

What does it mean if something is a performance? A performance is typically practiced, planned, and prepared. Public speaking performances can range from a speech at the Oscars to a line-lead discussing work with his employees. Regardless of the context, public speaking is elevated with self-confidence.

Public speaking shows a type of self-confidence. The need for public speaking will always be important for directing, leading, and developing people. Your presentation is one of the most important parts of your speech. Not only will people be paying attention to you, but they will be watching your presentation as well. There are many ways in which you can create a successful performance.

Before you dive into the P's of performance, you must focus on mental work. In this stage, you want to visualize what your presentation is going to look like. You can visualize a successful presentation and everyone standing and cheering when you're done. Imagine yourself being successful and build around that visualization. Now, move into the P's of performance.

- The first P is **planning**. As it suggests, during this stage, you plan your performance. From start to finish, left to right, you need to have it planned out. If you fail to plan, then you plan to fail. So, it's very important to prepare for a public presentation. Planning for a presentation means finding sources for making the presentation, finding online platforms to learn, asking others for advice, and planning the structure for the presentation.

> i. Planning for the structure of the presentation means creating an outline for your speech. (We will learn more about a speech outline later in the book.) You decide what parts of information will go in the introduction, the body, then the conclusion.
>
> ii. Plan on what you are going to do so you know what you need. Plan what you need to wear and look into the weather/conditions of the physical location. Plan where you're going to be and how you're going to get there.

- The second P is **preparing**. The general rule is there should be an hour of preparation time for each five minutes of the preparation. So, if you're going to have an hour presentation (60 minutes) you need to prepare for roughly 12 hours. When preparing, think of all parts of your speech. What are you going to do during, before, and after? Get any supplies you came up with during your planning stage.

> i. For example, if you're going to do a demonstration speech on how to make a free throw, then you will need a basketball,

tape (for the floor), tennis shoes, and whatever else you decide you want to use.

- The third P is **polishing**. Polishing is what can make your presentation stand out from others. If you just plan and prepare you can be good, but polishing can make your presentation great. Polishing can give your presentation a makeover and improve your self-confidence. You can use anecdotes, figures and facts, quotations, scenes from movies, news articles, brain teasing questions, and more to make your presentation stand out.
    i. When polishing, remember to polish without affecting the structure of the presentation or the basic purpose. If you do this, then you need to restart at the planning level.

- The fourth P is **practicing**. Practicing over and over allows you to get better and better before you have to deliver the presentation. It's not only important how often you practice, but how hard you practice. If you barely brush through your practice, then chances are you're going to (unconsciously) brush through your public speaking. Perfect practice makes perfect. Great practice means great results. Every great speaker you see today came from practice.
    i. You can use practice in your bedroom in front of your mirror, or practice in front of a group of friends and/or family. You can also record or video you speaking your presentation then listen or watch it.

- The last P is **presenting**. Speaking with confidence and a smile are two of the biggest elements you need for a successful presentation. When you're presenting your public speaking project you want to focus on the tone of your voice, modulation, body language, face and body gestures, and eye contact. You can study and use these presentation skills to practice your delivery.

  i. This particular part of the P's includes the final delivery of the presentation. You can take your planning and your preparation and your practice, finish it all up by polishing it, and then present it. If you're at the point where you present it and you don't feel sure of your project, go back through some of your previous steps and see what you can do to make yourself more confident and feel more secure about your project.

Just because these are five of the basic P's doesn't mean there aren't more aspects to improving your performance. Some other important P's include:

- <u>Persuasion</u>. Not only do you need persuasion if you are delivering a persuasive speech, but you need to persuade your listeners to listen to you. You have to provide them with enough reasons why they should be listening to you. You want to make your speech inspirational and convincing.

- <u>Passion</u>. When you have passion while delivering your speech, people are going to be able to notice. When you speak with passion you are a more entertaining speaker. You speak with purpose and your passion motivates others to listen to you when they can see it. Your ultimate goal is to transfer your passion into your listeners.

- Personal. If you can make your project personal, then you have a better chance of connecting with your audience. Making a project personal also means making it personal to yourself. You are going to be the one delivering the speech, so it's important to make it personal to you.

- Pause. An appropriately placed pause can make a really great performance, especially those with public speaking anxiety. This gives you time to think while you pause. Make sure not to pause too long or you risk losing the attention of your listeners. Also don't pause too long that you forget your train of thought or what you were going to say next.
  - o Using a pause at a bad time can take away some of the credibility of the speaker. It may make it seem like you don't know what you're doing, you're lost/unprepared/confused, or you're trying to fake your way through.
  - o Using a properly placed pause can increase the fluidity of your speech, reduce the stress, and make it sound better.

Presentation

Sometimes when you hear the words "give a presentation" you might feel nauseous. People immediately start to sweat and fidget. A lot of people may actually avoid something if it means they have to give a presentation. A lot of people make mistakes when giving a presentation simply because they are preoccupied with their fear or anxiety. Regardless of what you are talking about, how you give a presentation will affect your public speaking experience.

First, when you're giving a presentation, you want to make sure that you look the part. Dress appropriately for your setting. Don't wear a prom dress to give a speech at the park and don't wear a T-shirt to give a speech at a graduation. You want to look clean and appropriate so it improves your credibility with the crowd. The way you dress can affect your relationship with the audience. You can use your appearance to connect with your audience. If they relate to what you're wearing, then chances are they will relate to you.

You also want to make sure that your clothing is not going to distract you while you are speaking. If your pants are too tight or you are wearing itchy sequins, then you're going to be more focused on what is on your body rather than what you are saying. When you look good, you also feel good. And when you feel good, you look good. So, make sure not only is your audience comfortable, but you are comfortable as well.

Second, you are going to want to move around and use the space around you. Now we may not always have a lot of room to move when we speak, but generally we will have a small area that we can move around in. If you stand in one spot constantly for the entire speech your audience can get bored. Have you ever wondered why the camera angles change so much during a movie or TV show? It's been shown that when there is a constant change of picture or angle, it is easier to keep the attention of the viewer. If you are able to move around, you can engage your audience as they listen and watch you move.

Moving around can also show that you are confident. It can help you feel better about yourself, and it can move out some of your nervous energy. If you feel like your hands are trembling, then maybe stepping back from the podium and taking a few steps around can get your blood pumping. Standing in one spot for too long is also uncomfortable and can make you more focused on your discomfort instead of your audience. Your audience may also be able to pick up on the fact that you are uncomfortable.

Third, the use of hand gestures and body language goes a long way. People are 12.5x more likely to listen to body language than they are verbal language. This is because body language is harder to hide than verbal language. It can be easier for us to verbally lie, instead of physically lie. This is because our body language is innate, and sometimes we don't know it's happening. A lot of times we cannot control it. It is used by our body to express ourselves. Because we cannot always control our body language, people are more likely to listen to it because it doesn't generally lie.

Using your hands can help you get the thought out of your head. It can also allow you to move seamlessly through points as you use your hands to sort of guide your audience through what you're saying. Using hand gestures also keeps your audience engaged. It can help you get your point across.

Fourth, if you are using visual aids in your presentation, make sure they are clearly seen by everyone. If you are using a PowerPoint, make sure that you have a strong projector, a flat surface for the screen, and preferably the ability to dim the lights. PowerPoints can be seen in normal light, but they are better seen under dimmed lights. If you are using a laser pointer, make sure that it has batteries and back up batteries. Make sure you keep your laser pointer pointed at the floor when you aren't using it, so you don't accidentally shine it in someone's eyes. You can also make sure that you have batteries for a clicker if you are using it to move a PowerPoint slide.

A clicker can be beneficial for moving the PowerPoint slide without you having to stand at the computer or projector. With a clicker, you are able to move around the room and engage with the audience as you click through the slides. With a laser pointer, you are able to point to something on the slide without having to step in front of the projector. If you are trying to point to something, then you are probably going to be standing in someone's way. Using a laser pointer allows you to show what you are talking about without having to block the view.

Fifth, make sure you use your face. Smile, frown, blink, wink, etc. The more animated your face is, the more likely your crowd is to pay attention. If you look bored, you are going to make them bored. Make sure to control your facial animation, so it doesn't distract your audience. Yes, everyone is more attractive with a smile. Smiling also secretes important hormones in the brain that are responsible for happiness and stress relief. If you smile to impress your crowd, you could even make yourself happier.

You want to make sure that your visual aids are going to be seen by everyone. This means people in the front and people in the back. Depending on the size of your audience you may be able to send some visual aids around for everyone to see. You may also use handouts that can be given at the beginning or the end of the presentation. You are also a visual aid, so make sure you have some sort of stage or area to elevate yourself if you are in a crowded setting.

Make sure the lights are bright enough for them to see you if they need to and also if they need to read or take notes. Make sure there isn't any strong sunlight distracting people by shining in their faces.

During a presentation you also want to focus on your voice. You want to articulate enough so that people can understand what you're saying. Being clear and concise in your words may delete any confusion the crowd could have over what you're saying. You may also have bilingual individuals in the crowd, so enunciating your words can help them understand. This may be beneficial for those people who are hard-of-hearing as well.

Also control your tone and volume. If you are in a large area, it is important to speak with a high volume. Same goes with a small audience. How you say something is just as important as what you say, so make sure your tone is appropriate to the setting and topic. You don't want to have a know-it-all attitude or a condescending tone.

PowerPoint

Making a PowerPoint presentation can be very beneficial for your speech. Your PowerPoint presentation gives your audience something to look at while you are giving them information. If you are simply telling them something, they may not understand as well as they could if you had visual aids for them.

PowerPoint is a great program that you can use to create a visual presentation for your crowd. PowerPoint offers various slides, ideas, colors, formats, fonts, schemes, transitions, and more. A PowerPoint presentation can elevate your speech from good to great. Using a PowerPoint allows you to take a break from the audience's eye. It can also spark more attention from the audience so they can hear it and see it. Now there is more of a chance that they are going to retain it.

A PowerPoint presentation normally starts with a title slide. The title slide will have a large box for the title and a smaller box for the author (that's you). You can leave it blank, or you can change colors for each slide. It looks neater if you keep the same color scheme throughout, but creativity is the key here. You can also put pictures on your slides and arrange them with other shapes.

You can center the title and author boxes with the use of the program, or you can move and drag them where you want. PowerPoint can provide formatting throughout your presentation with a title box at the top and a box for text on the bottom. These boxes will be outlined when you click them so you can see what will go in that box. Each slide can have pictures, text, blank space, colors, YouTube links, and more.

You can also use transitions between slides. These transitions can make it more visually pleasing between slides. You can have one slide fade into another. We can have one slide blowup and another one pop up. You can even have them slide side-by-side like you would see in an older projector. These transitions can be a fun spin on a basic presentation.

Many times, at the end of a PowerPoint presentation, you can include some sort of references slide. This is where you can list any sources of information, any places that you got pictures or ideas, or resources for your audience to use for more information on your topic. The conclusion slide can also include the ending of your speech and make it more memorable. You could end with a large quote on the slide, a large picture, or an overall summarization of your speech.

When you are making a PowerPoint presentation, it's important to focus on the 5 x 5 rule. The 5 x 5 rule states that a slide will have no more than five words in each line and no more than five lines. You want to use your PowerPoint presentation as an aid to your presentation. You don't want to act as an accessory to your PowerPoint presentation. Keeping these slides symbol allows your audience to keep up with you but ensures that they are getting their information from you and not from the slide. It can also be intimidating and overwhelming for your audience if they see hundreds of words on the screen and they are expected to read it while still listening to you and possibly taking notes.

PowerPoint presentations are important for keeping your audience on track and helping them with notes, if they want to take them. Everyone's mind wanders. It's inevitable. But if you use a PowerPoint, then your audience can look back to the screen and get back with you instead of waiting for you to introduce the next topic. This means they spend less time confused and more time following you.

Don't get hung up on your PowerPoint, however. This is simply something you can use to help get your point across. You want it to be attractive, but you don't want it to be overly flashy. If it's too much on the eyes, the audience may not be able to focus.

If you are going to use PowerPoint, make sure you have all of your resources. This includes your laptop or computer, any cables you might need, a flash drive, power chargers, and time before the speech to set it up and test it. You don't want to spend the first five minutes of your speech trying to figure out why the projector won't turn on. This can waste the audience's time and energy, so when you finally start, they will be less likely to listen.

Chapter Four: Speech Writing

Speech Openers

One of the best determinations of how your speech is going to go is the opener. Your speech opener is the first impression you make on your audience. One issue you should avoid when beginning your speech is to call attention to technical aspects.

This means mentioning how bright the lights are, or if the microphone is working or not, or if your PowerPoint presentation is frozen, etc. If you draw attention to your technical aspects, whether they be broken or fixed, it's all your audience is going to be able to think about during your speech. One way to avoid this is by arriving early and double checking the tech before you get started.

Another way to avoid starting your speech is by mentioning how nervous you are. If you mention how nervous you are you can lose some of your credibility with your audience. They want to believe that you are almost an expert, or at least a master, in your speaking topic. If you mention how nervous you are this may show you have self-doubt, which can then in turn caused the audience to doubt you. This can also bring attention to how nervous you are, so the audience has a harder time listening to you because they are more focused on how nervous you are.

Speaking about how nervous you are can also make you more nervous. Mentioning how nervous you are can also make your audience nervous. This means that they will spend their time looking for cues that you are nervous instead of spending time listening to what you are talking about. While some people find it endearing and charming that you are nervous, it can actually distract them more than charm them.

Don't start with a halfhearted welcome. Your listeners want to feel like they are appreciated and that you are happy for them to be there. If you show them, you are happy that they are there it can make them happy to be there. A full and exciting welcome can also show that you are excited to speak about your topic and it can make them excited. If you say you're happy to be here but you don't actually look like you are happy to be here, you can confuse your crowd and make them think you are fake.

One of the best ways to start your speech is by telling a story. An interesting story will catch your listener's attention so that way you can use their attention to start your speech. You can start your speech with a story about the reason why you are there, the best or worst thing that happened to you, or a fictional once upon a time story. A good story can provoke emotions from your audience. It can make them feel with you.

Another great opener for your speech is starting with a big idea. If you are trying to solve a problem, and you have a solution, then you can open your speech with that solution. This might be a new idea to your listener, so once they hear it, they will be intrigued to hear more. Make sure your big idea is related to your topic.

You can open a speech with intriguing content that leads to curiosity. You can also start your speech with a joke or some humor. Humor can lighten the mood of your audience. It can destress them and lighten the tension in the room. If you can get your audience laughing, then you can get them relaxed. If you can get them relaxed, then you can get them to listen.

One great way to start out your speech is by using a thought-provoking question. You can ask your audience a question and then give them a few moments to think about it. You could have them raise their hand or just sit silently. This will get them involved at the very beginning and they will feel involved for the rest of the speech. You can start your speech with:

- "Did you know. . ."
- "Have you ever wondered. . ."
- "Do you worry about. . ."
- "Have you ever thought of. . ."

Creating a Speech Outline

A speech outline acts like a blueprint for a house. It will structure and organize your speech, so you can deliver it more clearly. It can take one small topic and expand it cover your entire presentation. When you're writing your speech, you want to start with the purpose. Once you have the purpose for your speech you know how to structure it. You will state your purpose in a "To. . ." statement.

- "To inform my audience. . ."

- "To persuade my audience. . ."
- "To demonstrate to my audience. . ."

You get the idea. You will not speak out this sentence during your speech. You will just use this statement as the structure for your outline. It's important to make sure that your purpose statement is specific and narrow and that you can also stay within time constraints.

You are also going to want to focus on the central idea. The central idea is pretty much your thesis statement. This is what you want to cover over the entire speech in one simple sentence. Your central idea could be stated, for example, as "The top three greatest hotels located in Los Angeles."

The overall outline should be labeled with the introduction, body, and the conclusion. These sections are segregated throughout the outline to keep your speech organized. In these sections, you can decide what information you are going to say and when you are going to say it. It will also make sure that you have all the parts and help you find where you are when you are speaking. You see, outlines can be used when giving a speech. So, the more organized they are, the more organized your speech will be.

Make sure you use the same indentation and symbolization for your speech outline. This makes it easier for you to find certain parts in your outline. It can keep your thoughts organized and give you a quick at-a-glance method. You don't want to have to look for the formatting, you want to look at the words. Most of the time, main points are shown with Roman numerals at the left margin. The sub points of the main points are shown with the capital letters A, B, C, D, etc. They are usually indented in the left margin five spaces. The sub points are written with 1, 2, 3, etc.

When you are making your outline, you want to state subpoints and main points in full sentences. When you put random words or vague labels in your outline it's going to be hard to show the content of your speech and what you want to tell the audience. You can prevent omission of your important information and fully develop your ideas when you use full sentences for main points and sub points.

An outline isn't a complete copy of your speech. Your outline is simply the bones of what you are going to say. Here is a sample:

<u>A Speech Outline Format</u>
Specific Purpose: (This is what you want to accomplish.) To inform my audience of the best hotels in Los Angeles.

Central Idea: (Summary that is one-sentence covering the key points in the speech.) Three of the best hotels in Los Angeles.

INTRODUCTION
I.   Attention getter. (This is something you are going to say to get the attention of your audience. You can use a story, joke, fact, etc.)
II.   Relate to the audience. (This is where you want to build a rapport with the audience. What do they like? What do you have in common?)

III. Establish Credibility. (Do you look confident? Do you know what you're talking about? You will want to include a sentence or two about your credibility.)

IV. Central idea and a brief description of main points.

BODY

I. First main point.
   A. First subpoint to your main point.
      1. Elaboration on your main point.
      2. Elaboration on your main point.
   B. Second subpoint.
      1. Elaboration.
      2. Elaboration.

II. Second main point.
   A. First subpoint to your main point.
      1. Elaboration on your main point.
      2. Elaboration on your main point.
   B. Second subpoint.
      1. Elaboration.
      2. Elaboration.

III. Third main point.
   A. First subpoint to your main point.
      1. Elaboration on your main point.
      2. Elaboration on your main point.
   B. Second subpoint.
      1. Elaboration.
      2. Elaboration.

CONCLUSION

I.   Show that you are finishing your speech. (You can say things like "In conclusion" and "To recap.")

II.   Summarize your main points and restate the central idea.

III. Choose a memorable ending.

This outline can be used when you are writing a speech. You can also use the outline to make notes for your speech. A lot of times as a public speaker, you can use notecards or other notes that you have created to use throughout your speech. Notes are beneficial for keeping you on track and making sure you don't leave out any important information. You don't want to load your notecards with information for fear of forgetting them because then you are going to have to pause too long to read the card, and it can hurt your credibility. Plus, it can get really stressful trying to speed read while there are people looking at you and waiting for you to speak again.

Normally when you are making notes, you just want to write a few words to keep you on track of what you're saying currently. The notes can also use transitions that you use in between your points. If you state each point on its own it can look choppy, and the speech will not be as smooth as it could. Putting transitions on your notes can allow you to seamlessly flow from one point to the next. Having these transitions can also keep you from abruptly stopping. When you see the transition on the note card, it will also give you a hint as to what is on the next card.

You can take notes on a piece of paper and have them with you, or you can use notecards. A piece of paper, such as the outline, may be simple and easy to keep up with because it is one sheet. However, you must keep eyes on where you are on the sheet. You also may have to look through your main points and sub points to ensure that you hit every part before moving to the next part.

Some people like to use notecards because they can focus on one thing at a time. One risk of using notecards, however, includes having them fall and you having to pick them up separately during your speech or you getting them out of order. If you accidentally mix your conclusion note card into the note cards of the body, then you could be thrown off and end up looking silly.

Some people number their notecards in the corner and make sure they are going in order. This can help you keep track of what number card you are on and how many you have left. This may distract you, however, from what you are saying because you are thinking about what you have left to say.

Notes are important, but they aren't mandatory. Even if you believe you know your speech from left to right you can step in front of those people and forget everything, or something unexpected could happen, and it could throw you completely off your game. Having notes ready, even if you won't use them, is always important for ensuring you will have an organized and information-filled speech.

Time Constraints

In a lot of public speaking scenarios, you will have a time constraint. Unless you are taking part in a filibuster, you are going to want to make sure that you get in all of the information that you want to during the time you are allowed. One way to make sure that you are going to stay in your time constraint is by practicing your speech while timing it. This doesn't mean reading it while there is a timer going in the background. This means standing up and pretending there is a crowd in front of you (or having an actual crowd) and timing yourself while delivering the speech exactly like you plan to.

Having an outline and notes are also important for making sure you stay in your time constraint. It can be easy to get off track or be distracted by something. Having an outline will make sure that you are moving through your information without spending too much time on any one part.

Having a time constraint may seem daunting, but it allows you to get down to the nitty-gritty in your speech. You may not have time for all these stories and anecdotes and riddles, but you will have time to deliver the most important parts of the information. Now this is not to say that you cannot include stories and anecdotes and riddles, but it just means you need to balance them appropriately with your information.

Time constraints also help you break your speech into parts. You can say you were going to spend 5 minutes on the introduction, 30 minutes on the body, and 10 minutes on the conclusion. You can split up the time to make sure that the most important parts get the most amount of time.

Chapter Five: Confidence is Key

Confidence is one of the biggest factors that can make you a good public speaker. You can build your own confidence to use as a foundation to being a good public speaker. Developing confidence can take time, it won't happen overnight, and it more than likely won't be easy. However, confidence is important and once you build it you can change your life.

Confidence can help battle our anxiety and uneasiness. It can keep us from telling ourselves that we're going to fail. When we know we are going to do a good job, then we have less anxiety about the outcomes. Anxiety is simply the fear of what can happen. We can use our confidence to fight this anxiety and fear.

Being self-confident means believing in yourself and your abilities. Confidence is one of the hardest factors among living creatures. Sometimes people are overconfident, and sometimes people have no confidence. While having too much confidence can be risky so can having no confidence at all. There are different ways, however, that you can build your confidence.

1. You can make a list of what you like about yourself. This list can be physical, mental, emotional, spiritual, physiological, etc. It will include everything that you like about yourself and what makes you happy when you think about it. Do you love your hair? Write it

down. Do you love your accent? Write it down. In love with your smile? You guessed it, write it down.

2. Sometimes it can be hard for us to make a list of what we like about ourselves so you can also make a list of what other people have told you they like about you. Think of when you have been complimented on your behavior or your outfit or a success. Do a lot of people comment about how pretty your eyes are? Have you been told multiple times that you are really smart?

    a. In this list you can include any awards and recognitions you have received.

3. Set a goal and use it as motivation. Even if it's as small as drinking a glass of water a day. Every time you reach this goal, you are going to feel good about yourself. The more successes you have with goals, the more confident you are going to be. As you keep reaching the smaller goals, start setting bigger ones. The bigger the goal, the more the motivation, the more success, and the more confidence you will have.

4. Some people may not be able to gain confidence on their own regardless of what they do, so seeing a therapist can always improve confidence. A therapist can allow you to work through some of your thoughts, anxieties, traumas, and troubles so that you have less noise inside your head. Participating in therapy can also show you that you aren't alone in a lot of your battles, and it can make you more confident in yourself because you see other people being successful.

5. Practicing can always help your confidence. You can deliver your speech to yourself in the mirror multiple times if you are nervous about other people seeing you. The more times you practice the more confident you

are going to be when giving your speech. Practice for confidence can be used in many areas of life. You can actually practice being confident.

    a. You can practice being confident by doing something as small as going to the store. You could wear a new shirt or a new style or simply walk around the supermarket like you own it. Pretend that you own everything in the store, but you are still being polite. If you practice being confident, you will eventually believe you are confident.

6. Learning more about yourself can make you more confident. If you learn about certain aspects about yourself and how they explain things that you don't like about yourself, then you are more likely to be patient with yourself. Being patient means not beating yourself up when you make a mistake. Sometimes when you make a mistake, your inner critic can tear you apart. When you are confident, you can step in and forgive yourself for your mistake. You can be honest with yourself that you made a mistake, but you can be confident in the fact that you will fix your mistake, or you won't let it happen again.

7. Physical appearance doesn't define who you are, but a lot of times changing your physical appearance can make you more confident. You can lose weight, dye or cut your hair, buy a new wardrobe, get a tattoo, or find another form of bodily self expression. Trying something new will allow you to express yourself and can then improve your confidence.

8. Positive talk with ourselves can be very beneficial. We are our harshest critic. Telling ourselves that we can do

it and that we are going to be successful can lead to us actually being successful. If we believe that we are going to be successful, it's easier to perform better. Something as little as looking in the mirror and saying "you've got this" can make your public speaking presentation phenomenal.

9. Helping other people can improve our confidence. Sometimes if we help other people, they will show their gratitude, and it can make us feel good about ourselves. As public speakers, we look to help others whether it be showing them, teaching them, or persuading them of something. The more we do for other people the more we believe in ourselves to be able to get stuff done.

10. Working out is a great way to improve confidence. Not only does exercise improve the healthy chemicals in our brain, but it can move blood throughout our bodies to collect and expel any toxins. These toxins can affect the way we feel and think. Exercise is physically beneficial as well as mentally beneficial. Working out can also make us feel good about ourselves and it can make us feel good too. This is going to help our confidence.

Confidence is so important because it can change our life. If we are constantly worried about what we are going to do about a situation or certain events, then our quality of life is going to suck. Being confident means we believe in ourselves to overcome any problems we may face, and this can stop the unnecessary worrying. This worry can be debilitating. We can use confidence to fight it.

One great way to develop confidence is to find out more about yourself. You can find out a lot about yourself through self-reflection. Know any times that you have been successful, or you have overcome a strong barrier. Thinking back on all the times you have avoided failure shows you what you are made of. Learning about yourself means knowing how and why you do the things you do.

Another way to learn about yourself is a personality test. Personality tests are great for explaining the reasons behind some of your actions. You may do things that you don't realize, and a personality test can bring a lot of these habits to your attention. These habits can be good or bad, so you can handle them accordingly.

Some great personality tests include:

- PersonalityPerfect
- The SAPA Project
- 123test
- Crystal
- MBTIonline

These are just a few of the personality tests that you can use to find out more about yourself. When you know more about yourself, you know your strengths that you can use during your speech (and the weaknesses you should avoid).

Strengths and Weaknesses

Knowing your strengths means knowing yourself. Self-awareness is when you realize and understand the reasoning behind your actions. You already know a few things that you're good at. You can make a full list to choose from when you're in a public speaking presentation. Self-awareness is a great tool that can elevate your performance.

When you know your strengths, you can exploit them during a performance. You can find your strengths by practicing for others. They can tell you the parts you completely nail and the parts where you need a little more practice. You can find your strengths by understanding what you enjoy the most. If you enjoy your presentation, then chances are you are going to be successful.

When you exploit your strengths, you are using them to your greatest advantage. For example, if you enjoy talking loudly, then volume would be a strength. If you annunciate very well, then speaking clearly would be one of your strengths. If you like to meet new people, socializing after the speech could elevate your public speaking presentation to a new level. You can make a list of your strengths and how you can use them.

If you aren't properly using your strengths, then you are wasting your potential. If you're using your strengths properly then you are enhancing your expertise and confidence. You will perform better and have a great work ethic. You will work with purpose because you know it's what you're good at.

Here are some helpful ways on how you can find your strengths.

1. Ask your friends what you're good at. They can typically notice things about you that you don't notice

yourself. Our friends and family can better realize our strengths because we are hard on ourselves. When we think we've done a terrible job, it may be great in reality, but we just don't believe.

2. Think of the times where you have been recognized, complimented, or rewarded based on a strength or performance of yours. Are you consistently told you're always on time? Punctuality is a strength. Getting compliments from your boss on the thoroughness of your work? You could be strong at attention to detail.

3. Correlate your thoughts with those who have complemented your strengths. If you have been told that you are honest, think of times in which honesty has rewarded you. Have you been in a situation where being honest has given you a positive outcome?

   a. It can be hard for us, sometimes, to believe others especially when they are complementing us. We may think that they are just being nice and not being genuine. However, when you can find real life examples that confirm your strengths, you are more likely to believe them.

4. Find out what you love. Chances are higher that if you enjoy what you're doing then you are likely to be better at it. You can be more patient with yourself and the task. You are also more likely to be more detail oriented and ambitious to finish successfully. When you know your passions and gifts, you can create a roadmap that exploits your greatest strengths.

5. Think of what gets you in the zone. If we are at work, we have those chances where we can completely submerge in work, and it seems as though time moves

around us. This is when you get on a roll or discover your flow state. This is a strong indicator that the task you are doing is one of your strengths.

    a. You know it is a strength because you were able to focus completely on it and work with little outside distractions.

6. Discover more about your relationship style. This can also go back to when we talked about the personality tests. When you understand the types of relationships and situations that bring out the best in you, you can discover your strengths.

Once you have found quite a few strengths, you want to figure out how to build your presentation around your strengths. Are you really good at event planning and venue finding? You can look for the opportunity to book and find your own public speaking venue. If you are good at sales, then a persuasive performance can be great for you. Find out your strengths, then find out how you can use them in your public speaking.

Knowing our weaknesses is just as important as knowing our strengths. This is because when we know what we are not so strong at, we can try to avoid that in our presentation. If one of our weaknesses is humor, then we may not want to go with an entertaining speech.

Finding your weaknesses allows you to be able to work on them, especially if they need to be incorporated with your presentation. If you need to be persuasive, then watch YouTube videos to study persuasive tactics. If you need to be entertaining for your speech, then watch some movies to get inspiration for jokes and puns.

Don't go deep into a rabbit hole trying to find your weaknesses to the point that you get discouraged with yourself and convinced you're not good at anything. Just pick a few of your obvious weaknesses and determine:

1. Do I need these in my speech?
2. Can I avoid them in my presentation?
3. What can I do to make them better for my presentation?

Knowing our weaknesses also teaches us a lot about ourselves. Do you seem particularly weak in one area? Is there a pattern in your weaknesses? There could be multiple reasons as to why we aren't good at something. Some of these reasons could be a simple fix. Our weaknesses can tell us just as much about ourselves as strengths can.

One issue with seeking others' opinions on our weaknesses is that we can become upset with others or ourselves. We can take their words personal and even hinder our views of them from now on. You'll always remember, "Well, Susan said I don't talk loud enough during meetings, so I don't want to be in any more meetings with her." It can also make us self-conscious of certain characteristics when select people are around. You'll think, "Susan is in here so I have to make sure that I'm screaming so everyone can hear me." You can put too much emphasis on fixing your weaknesses that you forget to use your strengths.

It's important to find a nice balance between strengths and weaknesses when delivering a public speaking performance. Too many strengths may change the presentation in a way that isn't what you're supposed to be delivering. Too many weaknesses can blow your entire performance. Focusing too much on your strengths can dilute your weaknesses and vice versa.

Make sure to challenge yourself without hurting yourself. Challenging yourself is important for self-growth and improving your weaknesses. Challenging yourself too much, however, can lead to self-destruction and a possible decrease in motivation and confidence. When you're trying to find and improve your weaknesses, there are a number of ways you can help yourself.

1. Admit you have weaknesses. If you're not willing to be honest with yourself, then you're not going to be able to work on the parts that need it most. Everyone has weaknesses; you just have to find yours, and accept them. Once you can get past yourself, you can change your life.
   a. Understand that working on your weaknesses is not about being perfect. It's about being diligent and becoming more well-rounded. Focus on your weaknesses as self-improvement projects.
2. Think of some areas where you know you need improvement. Also, consider areas where you want to improve.
3. Focus on the benefits of change. Change keeps things interesting. It keeps your attention in certain areas and improves your motivation.

When you see why it's beneficial to change your weakness, you're more likely feel the motivation to change.

4. Embrace the challenge of working on your weaknesses. Going into this with the right mindset will slingshot your productivity. Focus on this as a challenge, rather than a chore. Remember how much you have to gain.

5. Be consistent with yourself. Stay on yourself for working on your weaknesses. Believe in how much you can do and make the change. You might not see results overnight, so be sure to stay consistent in order to show progress.

6. Set goals when working on your weaknesses. Blindly working on them can improve them a little, but if you set goals, you'll be more motivated to accomplish them. Goals can prevent procrastination and allow you to work towards something.

Knowing how and when to use our strengths and weaknesses can improve our public speaking skills exponentially. They can help us create a strong presentation and explode our confidence. Using our strengths and working on our weaknesses are great confidence builders. Changing can be challenging, but the rewards are worth the work.

Chapter Six: Influencing Others

You cannot use coercion or intimidation when speaking to your audience and expect them to gain the intrinsic motivation to act on your words. Being influential means gaining admiration, trust, and confidence of those surrounding you. Influential people typically act deliberately.

Being divisive and sneaky won't increase your influence over others. You must be clear in your intentions, show appreciation for hard work, and give constructive criticism and feedback. You can also use direct influence, which can be voice to voice, face to face, or in other forms of electronic media.

Influence isn't magic. It won't happen in an instance and can easily be broken. When you move through life with a purpose, you have conscious thoughts about your actions and what others think of your actions. Influential people think of ways to improve and how to reach the goals they're aiming for.

It is important to influence others when you are speaking because you want them to *want* to listen to you. You can leave a better impression on them, and your words will linger in their minds. Being influential means being memorable. However, there are responsibilities associated with being influential.

You have to be a positive influence. When you are influential, people will look to you for direction, motivation, and advice. They will use you as an example when trying to make a decision. If you are being negative and leaving poor advice all around you, you are dragging others down with you.

You can accidently harm your followers if you don't understand the level of influence you have. You must pay attention to how influential you are over your listeners. Make sure you're being positive, even when you think no one is looking.

If you want to be influential, you need to listen and speak thoughtfully. You want to avoid drama and gossip, and focus on rising above and partaking in effective communication. Better communication increases your influence over others. This is because you are more able to accurately get your point across.

When you're influential, you take action. You don't get stuck by an unexpected situation. You move forward and find a way around your issues. Jumping in, when necessary, but thinking before you speak, shows you're eager to jump in and help.

Influential people tend to always be learning. They are constantly growing and learning so that others can look up to them. Keeping a mind that is accepting of new perspectives and ideas improves knowledge, acceptance, and understanding. They also exercise their brain and critical thinking, making them clearer to others. People who have high influence have tools they can use to adapt to various events and situations.

When you're influencing someone, you determine how easy or hard it will be for you to influence them next time. You must balance relationship building and getting results for effective influence.

Building Trust

Influence happens all the time around us. It can be making a connection, building credibility, or caring for a relationship. Influencing people means getting them to do what you want them to do because *they* want to. It won't be as genuine if they agree to your beliefs because they were told to do so.

Influencing others is important for public speaking because it can improve your performance. When you can better influence others, you have more positive outcomes. Your point in a speech is to encourage others to act. When you can better influence them, you can better convey your message.

Influence comes from trust in others. Trust requires building your reputation and building relationships. You want to give others a reason to trust you. In order to earn their trust, you must give them a reason to trust you. You can help others trust you by being true to your word.

If you say what you mean and mean what you say, others can see that you're genuine. When others sense a feeling of realness and transparency it can improve the trust in the relationship. It seems as though you have nothing to hide, and if you can bare it all to them, then you can better trust each other.

When you make a commitment, stick to it. Don't make promises you can't keep. You're going to be seen as unreliable and people will lose trust in you. When you make plans and stick to them, it can show your loyalty, and loyalty improves trust. When making commitments, make sure you're clear about the commitments; that way you're less likely to bail later.

Have great communication. When there is no question about what was said then chances are little that there will be a misunderstanding. The avoidance of misunderstanding creates a healthy environment for trust to grow. Good communication will also foster a great relationship.

Work on building trust over time. If you're too eager to gain someone's trust, then they might see you as fake or overbearing. People can get suspicious if you're trying too hard. Take steps in ensuring you create trust with another person over time. You could use this in your speeches by starting with your credibility, stating facts and clear ideas, and creating a connection with the audience. This will help you build trust throughout your presentation.

When building credibility, make sure to avoid self-promotion. This can make you look egotistical. When you recognize others, you can build good relationships. Instead of telling your crowd you won first place in a fundraising competition, talk about how much money you and your team raised. This focuses more on the positives while still highlighting your accomplishment. If you're specifically bragging about yourself, people can forget your accomplishment.

Avoiding self-promotion allows you to quiet your inner dialogue and focus more on those around you. When you're too focused on yourself, you can ignore the effect you are having on others. Listening to your crowd is a great way to gain information and insights that you otherwise wouldn't have gotten.

Don't expect a lot from the crowd at once. They are still sizing you up and learning about you. They are only a few minutes into your topic. This can be confusing or uninteresting to them at this point. Be patient and wait on your crowd to warm up with you. Don't panic or become frustrated when you don't feel an immediate connection with the audience. The trust will grow, you just have to give it time and effort.

If you are a repeat speaker, you will be able to build trust with a select audience that watches you speak more than once. If they see multiple performances by you, they will have a stronger sense of trust in you. Plus, you will be able to trust them more, too.

In order to build trust, you have to make careful and thoughtful decisions. Making decisions on the fly could lead to others getting disappointed in you. Think about what you might be saying "yes" to before actually saying it. Agreeing to someone automatically then having to cancel later can create an uncomfortable tension between you and the person you're making the decision with.

Be organized, so you can honor your commitments. Organization allows you to keep everything in one area. You can quickly access information you need before making a decision or forgetting a promise. Trust comes from the courage to say no to a wasteful decision or promise.

Understanding when to say no will keep you from becoming burnt out. Not only will it help you stay focused and productive, saying no will keep you from making careless decisions. You need to dedicate your time to things you need and want. Saying no allows you to create a happy balance, so you're not spread too thin.

Trustworthiness is built by consistency. When you're consistent, you're loyal. When you're consistent, you're reliable, and dependable. All of these qualities will create a trusting relationship.

Participate with everyone. If you are seen only conversing with a few people in your crowd, the others can seem more interested in those listeners than you as a speaker. You can build trust with the entire crowd by listening to them and providing appropriate feedback.

Being honest builds trust by showing your transparency and ability to be vulnerable. Lies will deplete trustworthiness. When people know you lie, or know you have lied in the past, they have a harder time trusting you in the future.

Helping people improves trust because people can detect authentic kindness. Authentic kindness will show people that you care, and that they can trust you. Being kind to your crowd, such as thanking them for coming, can improve the trust between you two.

When you show your feelings to your audience you are being open about your emotions. Showing that you care can increase the building of trust between you and your audience. This is built upon your emotional intelligence. Being emotionally intelligent allows you to understand the emotions of your listeners.

When you're focusing on your listeners, honesty is respected. Trust is harmed when you sacrifice your values. Make your listeners a high priority, so they feel included and approve of you. When your listeners feel heard, chances are higher that they're open to influences.

To see more about what your listeners are thinking and feeling, ask probing, thoughtful questions. This will bring out more emotions from the crowd. You want to understand their perspective so you can influence them the way you want to. Once you've made the effort to understand your audience, you will see what information is going to be the most important and the most relevant. This increases healthy communication between you and your listeners.

Communication

Communication can be defined as a two-way process where opinions, information, or thoughts are exchanged via symbols, speech, or writing. Delivery and acceptance of the information, as well as content and feedback, are vital for healthy communication.

Communication among humans is made up of three purposes: to relate, to inform or educate, or to influence. Communication is fluid and can change throughout the interaction. Communication, essentially, is the movement of information.

Influence in communication turns ideas into action and creates movement without command or force. Communication can be done without influencing, but you cannot be influential without communication.

Communication is a very important factor of influencing people. It's very important because you want them to understand what you want them to do. If they cannot understand your message, then all your other efforts will be wasted.

Communicating with people can be very different in various situations. It depends on the location, size of the group, ethnicity, topic, and so much more. There is a basic set-up that you can use as a general rule when trying to communicate an issue to others.

1. Describe what is currently going on. Discuss the current system, what it is, and how it works.
2. Make the problem statement. What is "wrong" with the system? What do you want to change about it? How can you make it different?
3. Create the outcomes. What do you want to achieve? What do you want the end product to look like?
4. Come up with a solution. Now is your time to brainstorm with others to make a solution, or pitch the solution you have already made. You can set and

describe the steps needed to solve the problem. Using a mutual perspective makes sure that all parties are heard.

5. Discuss the benefits of the solution to the problem. How can you work together to help the outcomes?
6. Get involved. Get the agreement and commitment of others. Work together to use the solution and solve your problem.

When you're accurately communicating, no one is worried about winning or who's "right" or "wrong". Communication is about reaching one another and solving problems. When you all work together, you can create a positive influence on each other.

When you accurately and quickly respond to solving problems, people will see you as a solution provider. This will make it easier for you to influence others the next time because they will want to hear what you have to say.

When you're communicating to influence others, such as in your public speaking presentation, remember these few tips to ensure you end up with great communication.

- Be clear in your message. Clarity will ensure there is no confusion, misunderstanding, or disagreements among the crowd.
- Be concise in your words. If you spend too much time rambling or hopping from subject to subject, chances are high that you can contradict yourself, say something you might regret, or repeat yourself. Just because you have a two-hour slot doesn't mean you have to

use the entire two hours, as long as you cover the agenda, and everyone understands. Plus, when you are concise, you are more likely to keep the attention of your listeners.

- Always be confident when you are communicating with others. If your listeners don't think you are confident in yourself, or confident in what you are saying, they are less likely to listen. When you are nervous as a speaker, you can distract the audience or even make them nervous. Keep relaxed, open body language and you will project steadiness and strength.

- Credibility is also important for proper communication. When you have good credibility, people are more likely to trust you. When they are more likely to trust you, they are more likely to listen to you. This means you're going to be able to influence them more easily as well as communicate with them.

- Be compelling. When you're speaking, you want to persuade or motivate people to listen to you. Not only do you want them to listen, but you also want them to act on your words. You can engage your crowd by showing value and then accelerating performance with your purpose and passion.

When communicating with others, focus on yourself as well as them. Make sure they feel heard and relieved. Keep in mind that it may take more than one interaction for proper trust building. As long as you show a genuine interest and put forth proper effort for healthy communication, then you'll be successful in your endeavors.

Leadership

Being a leader is a great way to influence others. Many times, people associate the word power with being a leader or having an influence over others. Is it *really* power, or is it influence? What do you mean by the word power? For example, being a manager means being able to hire and fire someone or change someone's schedule. However, being a leader allows you to help motivate and persuade people to make things better whether these things be in their personal life or in general life.

This is where the difference between authority and influence comes into play. You see, managers have authority over their employees. Managers have superiors as well, and it continues throughout a hierarchy. When you're dealing with influence, however, there are no statuses or classes. Having an influence on others is a quality that describes a leader.

Being a leader means genuinely caring about your followers. Your followers are just as important as you are, and without followers, there would be no leaders. Being a leader means looking out for others and helping them when we can. Leaders don't stray from challenge or fear and are willing to hold a lamp and guide others through a dark path.

When you are a leader, people tend to look up to you. Even if you don't know that you have an influence on others, they are paying attention to you when you are a leader. Being a leader means you are constantly watched by your followers. They look to you for guidance and advice and, if you are a good leader, they will trust you and you'll create a strong relationship.

It's important to have a strong relationship with your followers because nothing is impossible. The more people that you have working on something, the better chances are that it will come out well rounded. More people can weigh in on the solution, and you can come up with some creative ways to solve a problem. When you have a good relationship with your followers, you all can team up together and conquer the world.

Just like there is pressure associated with being an influence, there is pressure associated with being a leader. This is because being a leader and being an influence go hand-in-hand. In both cases, you have people who are going to want to seek you for help.

In order to be more influential, you need to be more of a leader. Now, you may think this is impossible because you are "just" an employee or "just" a person, so you can't be leader. People have a common misconception that there is only one leader at the top, and if you aren't at the top, then you aren't a leader. Leadership doesn't follow a hierarchy. It merely pertains to a person's actions, words, and characteristics.

Some common qualities in a leader include:

- <u>Being brave.</u> You have to be brave in order to lead others. You are normally the one going in headfirst; that way others don't have to. Not everyone has the courage to be a leader in all situations. There will come

a time where you have the opportunity to be a leader.
Be brave so you can put your followers at ease and be
an effective leader.

- <u>Being kind.</u> If you are a leader, you have an influence
over others. When you have an influence over others,
you take the risk of hurting them. They look to you for
help, and when you can't give it, it can harm your
relationship for next time. Being kind means you have
the opportunity to build people up. This is your chance
to help show them that there is good in the world and
that anyone can be kind. If you're rude, you could
break someone's spirit.

- <u>Being open-minded.</u> When you only focus on your
thoughts or opinions you are excluding everyone else.
Not only does this isolate them from you, but it also
isolates you from them. When you need them, you may
find that they won't be there. When you shut others
out and attempt to take all the glory and credit, it's
going to harbor resentment among your followers.
  - Being open-minded also shows your followers
    that you are willing to hear them and that you
    care about them. This creates a more effective
    and fruitful relationship.

- <u>Being inspirational.</u> Make people want to listen to you
and used your words. Motivate people from the inside.
This is called intrinsic motivation and can be one of
the strongest motivations that someone can have.

- <u>Showing passion.</u> When you show passion, you are
showing that you are genuinely happy and excited to
work on this topic or situation. Passion shows you're
prioritizing this task and you will do your best to

succeed. Passion also sparks passion in others, so it could spread like a wildfire.

When you're a leader, you understand there are certain pressures on you that aren't on other people. You realize there are people that look up to you, even when you're not looking. When you're a leader, you're influential. When you're influential, you're a leader.

Empowerment

If you want to influence others, empower them. Share your power when you can. Ultimately, you are all working together for the same goal. This is not to say give responsibility to others who cannot handle it or will handle it inappropriately. Not only will this affect you negatively, but it will also make them feel like a failure. Share power with those who will be successful with it. This creates a stronger bond between you and them. You'll build trust and experience with them, and both of you can benefit from the relationship in the future.

Empowerment is not always about giving power to others. It's about teaching others to empower themselves. When people crave love and affection from others, they tend to gravitate towards toxic people. These people give them just enough attention to keep them attached. This creates a really negative relationship because people are depending on others to make them feel better. When you put the power in their hands, they can find comfort within.

Saying things like, "I'm so proud of you," and "I think you're doing a great job," is motivational, kind, and very beneficial for a relationship, whether it be work or personal.

You can fully empower others by showing them they can make themselves feel better. Saying things like, "You must be so proud of yourself," and "What do you think about how great you're doing?" can cause people to look inside themselves when they need validation. You know the saying, "If you give a man a fish, you feed him for a day. If you teach a man to fish, you feed him for a lifetime". Telling people you are proud of them is like "feeding" them for that day. Teach them to be proud of themselves and they will "eat" for a lifetime.

When people need outside validation, they can turn into "yes" people. These "yes" people will do and say whatever they can in order to get the approval of others. This can be super debilitating and harmful to themselves. When you can empower people, you can have a great, long-lasting influence on others.

When you empower people, you have the opportunity to change their life. You can teach them to look within when they need help; that way they won't get lonely with themselves. They will be comfortable spending time alone and won't feel like they have to reach out for human affection. Empowerment isn't to replace human attention; it just takes the sting off of not having anyone for this attention. They can learn to give attention to themselves. This empowerment will allow you to have positively influenced them for the rest of their lives.

General Ways to Influence Others
"I've learned that people will forget what you said, people will forget what you did, but people will never forget how you made them feel." – Maya Angelou

The influences you have on others will last a lifetime. Whether it be good or bad, being an influence on others can be lifechanging. The way you want to influence others depends on your content, reasoning, environment, and other life factors. However, we have learned that there are ways you can improve your influence on others.

1. Give people what they want. When you give people what they want, they will return to you with a positive mindset. When you take a follower-focused approach, you're more likely to gain their approval and respect. Just like in public speaking when you give relevant and important information to the crowd, you are giving them what they want and what they need. If you are only focused on what you want, then you won't be able to focus on what your followers want. This will make it harder for you to reach your audience.

2. Make those around you feel important. People like to feel important. Without a sense of purpose, some may say their life is meaningless. When they feel important, they are more likely to gravitate towards the people who make them feel important. They do this because feeling important brings them happiness. They get the attention and fulfillment that they need in their lives. When you come in contact with these people, you are more likely to be able to influence them.

3. Show appreciation. Just like how people love to feel important, they love appreciation. If you show someone genuine appreciation for what that they are doing, chances are higher that they are going to complete that task more positively. You can't always force people to do something, and if you do, they aren't going to do it appropriately or to their fullest extent. They will harbor resentment against you and encourage them to do as little as possible.

4. Stir up the emotions of others. If you want to be influential, then it's important to connect with emotions. In marketing, many advertisements will use an emotional appeal to get the attention of their target audience. This emotional appeal draws people in and leaves a memorable commercial in their minds. This could end with the viewer buying or using the product. Targeting their emotions will ensure you leave a lasting impression on them.

5. Respect the opinion of others. Don't say, "No, that's not right," or, "That's wrong." Say things like, "Not quite," or, "I understand where you're coming from." Sometimes you will need to tell others they are incorrect, but *how* you tell them is just as important. They could be thinking differently than you. This means you could possibly benefit from their perspective, the same as they can benefit from the correct perspective. You both will be able to see the situation differently than you were looking at it before. Talking this out instead of

arguing about who is right and who is wrong will improve your overall understanding of the situation.

6. Show sympathy when dealing with issues and mistakes. People will make mistakes- it's inevitable. It is not your job to scold and attack them. It's your job, as a boss and a leader, to correct them. Teach them what they did wrong instead of yelling it at them and they won't be as hurt. Try to relate with others when they are talking about a mistake will show sympathy. It will give you both common ground you can use to ensure that the mistake doesn't happen again.

You can use your knowledge and experience to find opportunities to influence others. When you're in your day-to-day activities, look for opportunities where you can influence others. Remember, influencing others is not about taking control of them or having power over them. It means uplifting them and helping them.

Influencing Others Through Public Speaking

One of the best ways to influence others through public speaking is by being memorable. People will experience many, many public speaking presentations that they won't remember in the future. What you want people to do is remember you and your performance. When they remember you, you will have created a long-lasting type of influence. They will remember you and your content when they are reminded of it in the future. This could allow you to be influential even if you never speak to each other again.

As an example, think of a street performer talking about religion in the park. When you walk by, you can hear them speaking about their religion and what they think of it. If they are being boring, or not informative, or even rude and demeaning, they won't have any influence over you and your decisions. You will not be motivated to do anything with their words. Now, if that same person was reading real-life encounters with their religion, then you might create an emotional connection with one of the stories, especially if you had a similar experience. Creating this emotional connection can draw you into the speaker and make you want to listen to more. You may not exactly switch religions, but now you know more about that spirituality and that you can relate to it.

No matter the reason for your speech, you can influence others in general ways, the same as in general life, listed above. When you have a public speaking presentation, there are certain ways you can ensure you influence your crowd, regardless of the content or topic.

1. Create an emotional connection up front. The earlier you can provide an emotional connection, the better. Once a listener is emotionally invested, they are going to go to great lengths to make sure they are taking in your information. They aim to connect with you and believe they can benefit from your words. People can enjoy themselves a lot more when they have an emotional connection with the speaker. Targeting the emotions in your essay, whether they be positive or negative, will improve your audience's emotional investment. Making them feel a certain way

during the speech will help them remember the speech over the long-term. Encourage your listeners. Encouraging your crowd will show you believe in them. Acknowledge them, and reassure them that if you did it, then they can, too.

2. Use memorable facts and statistics. Try to find accurate information that isn't well known by the public. You shouldn't quote facts and sayings (too often) that everyone has heard multiple times. This can make you look generic or too lazy to do your own research. Giving these little-known facts can show others you are credible for doing your research. Because this information is new and interesting, chances are higher that it will resonate in the minds of your listener, even long after the speech. Teaching them something new will also help them remember your performance. They can say things like, "Oh well when I heard the speaker, I learned this." When they use that information in the future, there's a high probability they will remember your performance.

3. A persuasive essay is one of the most influential speaking presentations. During a persuasive essay you are trying to guide your audience to think one particular way about something. The best way to persuade someone is to influence them to make your desired decision. One great way to persuade your audience is to provide them with all of the

benefits they can gain from your viewpoint. You can talk more about the opposing side, or any negative benefits- that way they feel like they get the entire picture. If you tell people all good things only, they may think that it's too good to be true and won't give it a second thought. If you provide them with some risks and the opposing view, they may think that they are getting the whole picture and they are more likely to side with one side.

4. Entertainment is effective for helping you to influence your crowd. While you're giving your beneficial and interesting knowledge, give them some humor, too. Being funny will loosen up the crowd and entertain them. Being entertaining will make them want to listen to you. Using enthusiasm while talking and describing your words will also keep them entertained. Hand movements and facial expressions can show that you're enjoying yourself, and they will, too.

Influencing others is not always about them. When you influence others, you are reaping benefits yourself. When you positively influence others, you are leaving behind positive influence in the world. You may influence one person who, in turn, will positively influence the people they meet after them. Now you are not only influencing those around you, but you are also indirectly influencing everyone around them. Influencing others also provides a sense of fulfillment for you. When you can successfully influence others, you are living your life with a purpose.

It's important to influence others because the world needs positive people and positive influences. When you are a positive influence, you have countless opportunities to change people and change their lives for the better. You can leave the world behind you a better place knowing that you have positively influenced others.

Being influential also shows that you are confident and powerful. There are a number of characteristics that come with being influential and most of these are positive. These characteristics build your character and make you a more well-rounded person. When you open yourself up to influence others you also have the opportunity to be influenced yourself. We are never too old to stop learning and growing. Even though we think we may know everything about a subject, when we open up and let others influence us it can give us other perspectives that we wouldn't have known otherwise. The better perspectives we have and the more perspectives we have makes us have the opportunity to see the situation as a whole.

Chapter Seven: Stage Fright

Stage fright is exhausting. Not only are people trying to write their speech, study their audience, research their topic, and increase credibility, but they are also trying to fight their stage fright. It can be tiresome trying to fight away fear or hide it from others. This can definitely hurt your performance. Even if you have the perfect speech and the perfect audience, if you can't get yourself up on that stage, then all that work you've done is for nothing.

Stage fright can be debilitating. There are people who will completely avoid the stage at all costs. The thoughts of all eyes being on you is nerve wracking. People are terrified of embarrassing themselves and having everyone judging them while they try to give a performance. Actually, public speaking is one of the biggest fears among American adults. Many adults believe that public speaking is scarier than sickness, financial problems, flying on an airplane, and even death. It has been said before, "I'd rather be in my own coffin than give a eulogy". It seems to be over exaggerated, but many, many people feel this way.

Some will go their entire lives avoiding the stage. Whether it be something as small as delivering a message in a meeting at work, or as big as a TED Talk with 400 people in the audience, many people feel apprehension when they're getting ready to speak or give a presentation in front of a group. There are some people, though, that dread and even panic in these situations. If anyone is terrified of speaking in front of others, or being the center of attention, they could be a victim of social anxiety disorder, or a social phobia.

Avoidance is a coping mechanism that is used when someone is anxious about a situation or event. The people who use avoidance coping mechanisms consistently make excuses for why they won't or can't do something. It can be seen as procrastination, however, when people are specifically avoiding something because they are scared, it is considered avoidance. Avoidance is actually a lot more harmful than it is helpful.

Avoiding something won't always make it go away. If it is giving you enough anxiety that you feel the need to avoid it, then if you do avoid it, it will consistently sit in the back of your mind. When the thought creeps up, you'll feel that in the pit of your stomach and then fight to shove that thought back down. Not only are you avoiding the situation, but you are also avoiding your feelings regarding the situation. This is essentially just putting it off to worry about it another day.

Stage fright can cause problems with confidence and self-esteem. People can be really hard on themselves when they can't get up to speak in front of others. Some blame themselves for being scared and can go as far as leaving school or jobs because they cannot deliver a public speaking performance. Even the professional performers can still have trouble when getting ready to speak in front of people. It can be embarrassing when you are afraid to speak in front of others. Because of this, a lot of times people will try to keep the fact that they're scared a secret. It's important to understand that you can work through this fear instead of trying to hide it. You can also take comfort in the fact that stage fright will get easier as long as you work on it, and the more that you practice the easier it'll get.

In order to overcome your stage fright, you can perfect your public speaking skills, which can make it better. However, it won't fix it. In order to fix stage fright, you have to find the emotions and thoughts that are associated with your stage fright. Why are you scared to speak in front of other people? What makes you afraid of the stage? Are you scared of failing? Are you scared of judgement? You may say "It's because all of those eyes are on me." Well, why does that bother you? You have to get to the root of your problem so you can fix it.

In order to cure stage fright, you have to revise and address any negative beliefs, thoughts, images, perceptions, or predictions that you have related to public performing or speaking. For many people, stage fright is the fear of others laughing at or judging them. People care about what their audience thinks of them, and that puts a lot of pressure on them to do well which leads to stage fright. Being vulnerable, accepting yourself, and forgetting the idea that you have to prove yourself to others will help you cure your stage fright.

Stage fright can be especially hard for people who are already self-conscious or have previous negative experiences with public speaking. If you have had a bad experience in the past, you think that it will taint every experience in your future. It can be hard to see past that bad situation. If you are really self-conscious about the way that you look or the way that you sound you probably have a tough time getting in front of people at all. These are the negative thoughts and perceptions that we have associated with public speaking. We think "Well, what about last time?" or "What is everybody going to think about my appearance?"

It takes a lot of mental energy when dealing with stage fright. You are either flying through your thoughts and thinking of everything that can go wrong or spending every ounce of energy you have trying to calm down and fight this stage fright. By the time you actually get on stage and get ready to give your performance, you're exhausted. When you get mentally stronger, you will find that it's easier to fight these feelings.

It's important to learn some cognitive behavioral methods when you're feeling anxious. It's important to learn to calm yourself down because there may not be other people that can do it. While many people resort to medication or other natural remedies, this isn't a fit for everyone. Medication is great for some, but it could potentially leave your mind cloudy, and that makes it harder for you to give your performance. You can learn new skills that will help you combat your stage fright and help you come out on top.

1. Focus on the benefits of your performance. Are you going to make new friends or work connections? Are you sharing some really great content with your crowd? Are you getting some sort of promotion or recognition by doing the speech? Instead of focusing on how scared you are, focus on how excited you are going to be for the outcome.
2. Understand that you are going to typically think the worst will happen. Do you think your pants are going

to fall down or your dress is going to fly up? You can just envision the crowd booing you off the stage as they throw old food at you. Anxiety is simply the fear of what *could* happen. Try to visualize everything that can go right.

3. Envision yourself being successful. If you see yourself giving a great speech, and everyone is standing in clapping at the end, you're going to feel more confident and excited when you go in to give your speech. You've already envisioned that the crowd loves you, so it's reassuring to your mind.

4. Fight thoughts that lead to low confidence and self-doubt. What if I didn't study enough? Did I write enough on my note cards? Don't hate yourself with these last-minute doubts and questions. Trust that you did a good job on writing your speech; now trust that you're going to do a good job giving your speech.

5. Find ways to calm your mind. Listen to your favorite song or do some quick meditation. Focus on your breathing, count to ten, and take five deep breaths. The idea is to get your mind to slow down enough for you to fight the stage fright.

6. Physically prepare for your speech. Eat a good breakfast, go for a walk, exercise the days before, etc. If you can better prepare your body for public speaking, you have better chances of preparing your mind. In order to prevent anxiety, try to avoid sugar, caffeine, and alcohol on the day of and before your performance.

7. Practice before you go on stage. Practice with your friends, your family, and even backstage with your notecards. Listen to your voice as you talk about your

speech. Pretend you're talking to yourself, or pretend you are talking to one person you know. Listen to the calmness and casualness of your voice. Try to remember that when you are about to give your presentation.

8. Do the Superman pose before your performance. The Superman pose is the idea that standing upright, with your chin in the air, your chest pointed out, and your hands on your hips (like Superman) will "trick" you mind into thinking you're strong, confident, fearless, and ready to tackle any event thrown to you. Focusing on the stance, rather than your own thoughts, can you help you redirect your mind away from those negative thoughts.

   a. Science shows that when you smile, even if it's fake, your mind will release serotonin. Serotonin is a neurochemical in the brain that is associated with happiness. So, if you fake smile long enough, there's a high probability that your brain will think that you're happy and ultimately make you happy. This is the same idea for the Superman pose.

   b. When you are giving your performance, try to sit or stand in an open and confident position. Hunching over, looking down, or having your arms crossed in front of your chest can show that you are in a defensive stance. When your body is acting defensive, it can tell your mind that you are being defensive. This can lead to more fear.

9. Stop trying to be perfect. People make mistakes- it's human nature. People get nervous- it's normal. Try not

to beat yourself up for being scared or for making a mistake. Chances are high that your audience won't know you've made a mistake unless you bring attention to it. If you leave out a part of your speech, try to fit it in another area. Don't stop and say, "Oh, wait, I forgot".

The ultimate goal of combating stage fright is trying to get it down to an acceptable level. You don't have to completely cure your stage fright, and let's be honest- some people never will. Even if they have given hundreds of performances before, they still may get a little nervous before going on stage. This is natural and healthy. You are not looking for a cure for stage fright; you are simply looking for it to be manageable.

You want to try to get your stage fright at an acceptable level before you go on stage. This isn't always doable, however, so our stage fright can come up and get on stage with us. One mistake, one mess up, one stumble, and we are falling apart in front of these people. For some people, their stage fright melts away as they speak. For others, it will bubble back up in times of silence or uncertainty.

Stopping for a question or comment can create awkward silence that can make our stage fright come back up. If someone is in the crowd and heckling us, it can give us such severe anxiety that we have to leave the performance. This is why it's important to have behavioral tools, to help keep us calm during the performance. We can always take a few deep breaths and continue.

If you feel yourself getting nervous on stage, try a few of these tips to calm yourself down and get back on track.

- Take some deep breaths- not so big that the audience notices and wonders if there's something wrong with you, but just enough to regain control.

- Plant your feet firmly on the ground. Imagine all 10 of your toes are outstretched and placed firmly on the floor beneath you. The thought of you being stable on the ground will center you and bring your mind back into that room.

- Focus on your presentation. It can be hard once you mess up or if the audience has done something to throw you off. However, jump right back into your content and keep going.

- Smile. Remember earlier when we said smiling would make you happy? Smile to your crowd and it will put you at ease as well as them.

- If it gets to be unbearable, try to focus on a break. Don't run offstage or panic. Pick something out of your topic and tell your audience to think further about it. Tell them to take a few seconds to think quietly about what they think or to lean over and speak to a neighbor about your content. Ask a thought-provoking question. Take this opportunity of silence to recollect yourself so you can continue your performance.

Physical Effects of Stage Fright

When you have stage fright, you are anxious. This anxiety causes symptoms to manifest in many ways. People see public speaking as an intense situation. When we are in this situation, our anxiety attempts to prepare us for the experience. In the short term it will increase your breathing and heart rate, and focus blood flow to the brain.

It's important to recognize when you are experiencing stage fright so you know how to fight it. If you are overcome with a headache and nausea, and you don't know why, it could be stage fright. Stage fright not only tears apart our mind but affects our body as well. Even if we can learn to control our thoughts, our bodies can still feel the effects of stage fright. Some people feel more physical symptoms than mental. Others may feel more mental symptoms than physical. Some can feel both.

<u>Mental Symptoms</u>
- Self-doubt
- Anxiety
- Sadness
- Avoidance
- Decreased confidence
- Increased speed and number of thoughts in your mind
- Inability to think clearly
- Difficulty focusing
- Poor memory

<u>Physical Symptoms</u>
- Upset stomach, nausea, stomach pain
- Diarrhea
- Headaches

- Trembling
- Muscle spasms, pain, and twitching
- Restlessness
- Inability to get comfortable
- Inability to sit still
- Increased heart rate and breathing
- Clenched jaws, fists, or muscles
- Neck/shoulder tension
- Lightheadedness/feeling faint

There are many activities and exercises you can use to calm both your mental and physical symptoms of anxiety. So, when you are experiencing the physical effects of stage fright, there are tools you can use to calm down.

- Ginger is a natural substance that works wonders for nausea and upset stomach. Ginger can be found as a tablet in the vitamin section or at your local pharmacy. Ginger allows for anti-inflammatory properties that can help with nausea.
- Stretching and exercise can prevent and resolve the side effects of physical anxiety. Exercise allows your body to burn up that extra energy that is created from being anxious. Stretching allows you to increase the blood flow to the muscles which allow you to relax. Muscle tension can cause pain and discomfort, and stretching can fix muscle tension.
  - When you are nervous you probably clench your jaw or your shoulders without

knowing it. After some time, the muscle begins to hurt and tire out because it has been flexed for so long. Stretching allows your muscles to relax which can, in turn, allow you to relax.

- Deep breaths are a great way to help both physical and mental symptoms of anxiety. The increased oxygen in the blood allows you to think more clearly and move easier.

- As funny as it sounds, chewing gum can actually help with anxiety. When you are chewing gum, your brain thinks you are eating. If you are eating, then your mind is focused on what's in your mouth. Chewing gum allows you to get out any extra energy you might have without needing to fidget with a pen or your fingers.

- Yoga and meditation can also be great ways to relax your body. The great thing about yoga and meditation is that you can do each of them for as long as you want. Meditation for five minutes could be just as beneficial as 15 minutes of exercise. 10 minutes of yoga could be the same as 30 minutes of meditation. You can find quick routines or podcasts that you can do or listen to before your performance.

- Getting enough sleep can be very beneficial for the physical signs of stress. Get a good amount of sleep the night before your performance so your body will have more energy to fight off the stress. This will lessen the effects of your stress, meaning you won't feel it as much.

- Physical touch can help some people with stress and anxiety. When we touch another person, our body releases oxytocin. Oxytocin is a neurochemical in the brain that is responsible for relaxation, human connection, and bonding. When we feel the touch of another person, it can be comforting. See if you can hug, hold hands, or simply stand near someone you know, love, or trust.

- Wearing comfortable clothing can help prevent the physical effects of stress. You won't have to worry about what you're wearing, or it being uncomfortable, or it being too tight. Clothes that are too tight can lead to more anxiety.

- Probiotics can be beneficial for anxiety and gut health. Taking probiotics can improve the healthy bacteria in your gut. Since your gut and your brain are connected, when your gastrointestinal health is good, your anxiety is likely to get better.

Stage fright is the thought of what could go wrong or what could happen badly while you're speaking or performing. It is the thought of being judged or watched by others. Stage fright is very common, but it can still be really hard to deal with. Now that you have the tools you need to fight stage fright, test them out. Practice out your speech on a handful of people you don't know or barely know. Volunteer to go up to the board during class. Stand and talk about your job duties in a meeting.

Chapter Eight: Mistakes to Avoid

Mistakes are going to happen in all areas of life. We can't always prevent them, but what we can do is learn which mistakes are avoidable. There are small, common mistakes that public speakers make. We can recognize these mistakes and learn from them. That way we won't repeat them.

Some simple mistakes that we can avoid as public speakers are listed below.

1. Reading out loud. This can be reading verbatim from notes or on a slide. Instead of just reading from the screen or cards, elaborate on them. Connect the material to your crowd. Weave in specifics to show your audience that you know what you're talking about. If you're just reading cards, then you crowd can feel disconnected from you.

2. Memorizing a script. If your performance sounds too rehearsed, people listening won't be able to hear your passion. You have to improvise a little when public speaking. This way, you look involved in that current environment, and you're not just repeating something you memorized.

3. Talking too fast or too slow. It can be easy to lose track of our speed when we get in the flow of talking. Talking too slow or too fast will distract

our audience. They won't be able to understand, and it will be hard to keep their attention.

4. Poor usage of PowerPoint slides. Putting too much information on one slide can cause the audience to read more than listen to you. You want to use the slides as an *addition* to your presentation, not as your *presentation itself*.

5. Using a monotone voice. Using a monotone voice can be boring and lose the attention of your listeners. Raising and lowering your tone and dialect when talking helps you entertain the audience.

6. Lacking facial expression. If you have a bland look on your face, it can seem like you're uninterested in your presentation. If you don't look interested, then how can you expect your crowd to look the same?

7. Fidgeting or pacing when you're presenting can distract the audience. It can also make them uneasy and cause them to fidget. Fidgeting and pacing can also distract you from what you're saying and show your audience that you're nervous.

8. Standing behind a desk or podium the entire speech can bore the crowd. If you move around the stage and show more of your body, the crowd is more likely to connect with you.

9. Avoiding eye contact shows signs of nervousness. When you're constantly looking down or in other directions, it can be hard to make a stronger connection with the audience. Being able to look them in the eyes will show them you're paying attention to them the way they are paying attention to you.

10. Lack of practice can almost always show when you're presenting. If you've practiced, you are going to look more comfortable, and your speech will go over more smoothly.

11. Going over on your time. You may be passionate and ready to talk all day. Chances are, however, that your audience doesn't feel the same. They may enjoy your performance but if they have plans after, or they're simply hungry and needing a bathroom break, it can get frustrating for your audience. After a certain time, you will either be asked to stop, or people will start gradually leaving.

These are just a few mistakes that you can make. But it's important to recognize them and make a plan to avoid them. Let's use the mistakes above as an example for making ways to avoid mistakes.

Reading out loud can be very helpful for practice, but you'll sound like a robot if you do it in front of people. It'll be hard to sound authentic. To avoid this, make note cards with the main points of your message. Don't write full sentences or else you'll end up reading them. If you lose your audience, it can be hard to get them back. Use the notes at a glance. You want to use them as a guide. Notes also prevent you from memorizing a script.

When you memorize a script for your presentation, you are too concerned with learning your lines than you are working on your non-verbal communication and presentation skills. Plus, if you skip a line or forget your words then you could be caught up and lose your place. Instead of memorizing a script, create a theme for your presentation and organize your ideas in chunks. Start the "chunk" with the main idea (remember the outline in the planning). Talk yourself through this subject and you'll make a more genuine relationships with the audience.

Talking too fast can make the audience switch off because they're not able to understand. Talking too slowly can also make the audience lose interest. You also risk getting out of breath, increasing your heart rate, starting to sweat, or increase your anxiety. Many people can talk too quickly when they want to hurry up and get their presentation over. This may seem enticing but speeding through it can actually make you more nervous and will affect your outcomes.

To better combat this, learn to be okay with silence. You don't have to fill every second of your presentation with noise. Silence gives you, and your audience, a break. We're all able to listen to ourselves. Silence allows your information to sink in with the audience. Plus, they get a little break from listening (and you get a break from speaking).

The poor use of PowerPoint slides can affect your presentation. When used appropriately, slides can help keep the attention of your audience, provide highlights, help tell a story, and give visual input to the people who learn the best that way. If you're not using your slides properly, you can focus more on them than the audience.

To use slides to the best of their ability, use a presentation clicker and keep it in professional view. This way you don't have to continuously look over your shoulder and back at your screen instead of the audience. You want your slides to be clean and visually appealing. Use colors that match and complement each other. A font that is large and easy to read is best. You don't want to use a small cursive font because your audience may not be able to read it- especially those that are sitting in the back.

For bonus points, you could print off your PowerPoint presentation and give it to your listeners. This way, they will be able to take notes on what you're saying. They will also be able to take the most important parts of information home, since your PowerPoint slides should have the most important points on it. Also make sure you're not standing in front of the screen or blocking any views of your audience.

Being monotone means speaking with only one tone and pitch. You don't change whether you're excited or you're angry. Despite the audience's efforts, if a speaker has a dull or boring voice it's going to be hard to pay attention. Use your voice to bring inflection, color, and character to the audience.

Before a performance, take a few deep breaths to calm your nerves. This can make your voice sound more natural and under control. Talk to your audience like you would your colleagues. Let your voice flow with your natural highs and lows in conversation. If you aren't sure whether you're monotone or not, record yourself while practicing.

Facial expression can make a big difference in your performance. Facial expressions can help ease those around you, help you connect with your audience, and allow you to better convey your message. However, when we're nervous, our neck, face, and jaw tense up. This can make us look blank or angry.

To help fight this, try to remember your facial expressions and remember to stay relaxed. If you notice your jaw is clenched, try gently biting the tip of your tongue between your front teeth. This allows your jaw to relax. Try to remember this feeling and recreate it when you think you might have a stern look. You can also smile while its appropriate. This can make your crowd smile, too! Smiling will also let you relax a little more and improve your mood.

Fidgeting and pacing can distract the crowd. Do you have any small expressions you use when nervous? Do you pick at your nails or play with your hair? Do you tug at your clothes or rock back and forth? You can learn to handle these reactions so they don't distract your audience. These small coping mechanisms can distract your audience and harm your credibility and confidence.

To fix these movements, plant your feet firmly on the ground. Imagine you are flattening your feet and all your toes onto the ground. Move your feet shoulder width apart and let your upper body relax. Focus on letting your chest and shoulders relax so you can breathe into your stomach. Move around but only with purpose. Allow your hands and arms to move naturally.

Don't stand behind a desk or some other form of stand. This can limit your non-verbal communication and show you're nervous or you don't want to be there. If you're leaning on it, it could look like you were forced to be there, you don't want to be there, or you're tired. Slowly and purposefully move around the front. Make sure you have a microphone so you can be heard clearly.

Avoiding eye contact can feel good when we're nervous. Looking high up or down low can ease our nerves since we can't "see" anyone. Eye contact is important because it helps you connect with your audience and build relationships. In order to improve your eye contact, pick a group or table and look the in their eyes while speaking. The listener will usually nod or smile to acknowledge you. Once you've gotten everyone at that table to see you, move to the next table. Make sure you're looking around, too. You don't want to stare at a table so long that others feel neglected.

If you aren't prepared for your speech, your listeners may be able to tell. It's important to prepare beforehand because winging it isn't professional. You will be less influential than you would have been if you had prepared. When you don't prepare, you can forget important parts of your presentation.

You can also look unprofessional, disorganized, and inexperienced. People are willing to give up their time for speakers, so we should make the effort to get organized and practice.

Practicing and preparing can be boring, but it can make a big difference in your performance. You can practice by recording a video of yourself, practicing in front of a mirror, or talking to friends and family.

If you use more time that was given to you, you could be embarrassed or not invited to come back and speak again. Spending too much time can also be inappropriate if you are a guest speaker. Cutting into another speaker's time is selfish and disrespectful. Your audience is likely to become aggravated with you and not trust you.

Plan your presentation out so you're unlikely to spend too much time on any one subject. Also, make sure you can see a watch or clock. This can help you keep up with the time. Make sure you allot time for questions and disruptions.

Mistakes can be personal to everyone. You are going to have certain risks that others won't, and vice versa. Identify specific mistakes you might make and how you can prevent them. Think: how have other people in your field have made mistakes public speaking?

Recovery

You're walking across the stage to give more attention to the other side of the crowd. You're smiling at the crowd and gliding across, using your hands to portray your message. All of the sudden, your shoe gets caught on the microphone cord and you lift your foot to take a step, but you can't. You come down on the stage and hear a gasp from the crowd. As you lay there, there's probably hundreds of thoughts going through your head.

Once we've made a mistake, our brains jump to ways to solve the problem. Do we lie? Hide? Deny? This is when we fight or flight. When we fight, we decide to stay there and work through. When we take flight, we run. Now, during a public speaking presentation it's not really appropriate to take off running. So, guess what? We're going to fight.

It's everyone's worse nightmare to make a mistake in front of people, especially when public speaking. When do you make a mistake, though, it's not the end of the world (unless you act like it). When we've made a mistake during a public speaking presentation, try to focus on how you're going to work through the problem.

> 1. Use humor. Draw attention to it. Make it into a joke. If you fall face first, just hop up and say, "Well, that wasn't supposed to happen until the end of the presentation". It'll lighten the mood. Plus, people are more likely to empathize with you and you all can move on.

> 2. Brush it off. Stand back up, fix your clothes and hair, turn to smile at the crowd, take a deep breath, then continue with your presentation. There is no need to call attention to it if you don't want to.

3. Involve the audience in moving past it. Turn to look at the crowd and ask, "Is my hair messed up?" Ask them to raise their hands if they're embarrassed, too, or if they've ever fallen in front of a crowd before.

4. Take a brief pause, if you have to. Simply stand up and leave stage to collect yourself. You can step out of the room, take a drink and a deep breath, then head back onto that stage as if nothing happened.

Don't beat yourself up and don't panic. Everyone makes mistakes. Just recover from them and move on. The type of recovery should vary based on the mistake. For example, if you stumble on your words or miss a part of your presentation, don't call attention to it. Many times, your audience won't recognize when you stutter or miss a part of your information. If you accidently say something inappropriate, it's probably not best to use humor.

Go with what feels comfortable at the time. Do you need to take a break, or can you crack a joke? This is how you can win back the crowd. Win your crowd back after a mistake so you can continue the presentation and finish strong.

Chapter Nine:
Telecommunication

Technology revolves through almost everything we do in our lives. From making a phone call to making a cake, technology is everywhere. Why wouldn't it be involved in public speaking?

When you think public speaking, you probably think of standing in front of hundreds of people and giving a presentation. Which, yes, that could be true. But you don't have to be standing, or even in front of hundreds of people, especially if you're giving a virtual public speaking presentation.

A virtual public speaking presentation is when you're speaking to a group of people through a computer, projector, tv, or other electronic device. Giving speeches verbally is interesting, but doable. It will take some practice, but you can be just as good of a public speaker in person as you can online.

First, make sure you have a stable internet connection. It's best to use a direct-wire connection. This means that your computer should have a hard-wired connection to the internet. Wi-Fi can be reliable, but not as strong as the hard-wired connection. When your internet isn't strong, it can cause issues with your entire presentation. Your audio, video, connection, and more will all be affected.

Second, have a good background. You want it to be clear and free from any mess or distractions. An open, clean, bright background will show you more than your environment. You want people to focus on you, not what's around you. A good background can also make you stand out. You'll be the center of attention.

Third, test your sound before you start. Make sure your computer or microphone is picking up your voice clearly. You don't want a bunch of noise and static breaking up what you're trying to say.

Fourth, make sure your lighting is at a good level. If it is too bright, it can make your picture look blurry and diluted. If it is dark, your crowd won't be able to see you. Having good lighting is beneficial to making you look better and letting the crowd see you better. A tip to having good lighting is to have a diffuser. This means something that keeps the light shining right on you. This can also lead to too much light.

You want a softer light, because that is going to look better on camera. You can reflect the light off of a wall or umbrella, so the light is delivered to you in a softer way. It's harsher when it's pointed directly at you. White light and daylight are the best options.

When you're giving your presentation virtually, take advantage of email. Send your listeners any notes or resources you'll be using. This way they can have the information before you start. You can also contact them about the presentation and anything they might need beforehand.

There are some programs that have a comment section while you're giving your speech. Your listeners will be able to leave comments regarding what you're talking about, and you can answer them at the end of the presentation.

Anytime you put anything online, it's there forever. Even if you take it down, if someone has it saved, you'll never be able to get it all back. When you're giving presentations online, be prepared for the chance that it will get recorded. Even if there is no need for it to be recorded, people still have the ability to record you online. There is still an issue with this in person, but it's easier for someone to do it on their device.

Troubleshooting

Technology can be tricky. It can be just as frustrating as it can be helpful. When you're having trouble giving your online presentation, there are a number of things that can go wrong. Regardless of the device you're working on, try these troubleshooting tips.

1. Restart your device. You're likely giving a presentation on a phone, computer, or tablet. Try turning the device off then back on again.

2. Disconnect from the internet, then reconnect. If you're using Wi-Fi, turn the Wi-Fi off and back on. If you're using an ethernet cable, then unplug it and plug it back in.

3. Close out and reopen your program. If you're using Zoom, quit the program and reopen it.

4. Try different headphones or devices. If you're having trouble hearing others, and they're having trouble hearing you, try a different set of headphones/a different microphone. Trying another device may also help with your issues.

5. Use a different web browser. You can use Google Chrome, Safari, Firefox, or other web browsers. Normally you can find a list of approved web browsers on the website of the program you're using.

Have your listeners troubleshoot on their end. If they're having trouble hearing or seeing you, have them try the tips above. Chances are if both of you are having issues, one of these tips are likely to fix the problem.

You can send the list of troubleshooting tips to your listeners before your presentation. That way they can perform any troubleshooting before the presentation begins. Now they won't have to miss any of your presentation fixing their problems.

Be sure to include time for troubleshooting at the beginning of the presentation. If you wait until the beginning of the presentation to start, you may experience issues with your technology. This is frustrating and distracting. By the time you get it fixed and get started, you'll be late and flustered. Your crowd will be distracted and annoyed as well.

Audience

Dealing with a virtual audience can be tricky. For one, you aren't really able to tell if they're paying attention – especially if they have their camera turned off. When you're using a video-conferencing program, you and the viewers can both have your audio and cameras on. You can choose to mute the viewers or keep them from opening up with their camera.

However, when given the option to open the camera, many times the viewer will choose to leave it off. Viewers are more comfortable when others cannot see them. This can have effect on you, the speaker.

If you cannot see your audience, you may feel like you're talking to a blank screen. This can be good for those who are nervous about people speaking. However, when we speak to a black screen, we aren't able to take in any feedback from the audience.

We get both verbal and non-verbal feedback from the audience. Without this feedback, we may not know what the audience is thinking. Without the continuous feedback, it can make us unsure about how we are doing. This means we have to get feedback other ways.

In order to get feedback from your audience without seeing them, utilize the comment or chat feature. Take a second for the audience to send any chats to each other, or to you, when you ask questions.

You can also email your viewers with the opportunity to complete a small survey or share any thoughts or comments with you. Not all of your viewers will do this, but the ones that do can give you appropriate feedback for you to use next time. This feedback is helpful in the long-term rather than the short-term.

Without feedback from the audience, we don't know how to adapt our presentation to fit the needs of our viewers. We aren't able to tell if they're bored, interested, engaged, lost, confused, etc. We can't use their facial expressions and body language to determine what they need.

In this case, you could ask for the viewers to unmute their mics and talk to you about your topic. You could take a second to see how they feel and adapt to your presentation. Encouraging your audience to turn on their cameras at the beginning of the presentation can help you get this visual feedback you need to fine tune your presentation.

Without a camera, you're not really sure if they're paying attention, either. If they have their camera and audio turned off, they could be nowhere near their computer- but keep your confidence and speak like they're sitting right in front of you.

It can be easier for people to speak online than it is in person. It's less intimidating when you don't feel everyone's eyes on you. Some people may opt to give an online presentation rather than an in-person presentation.

When you're speaking to people online you typically need a more engaging speech to make sure that people are paying attention. When people are watching a presentation online, they likely have more distractions than they would have in person. Some of the viewers will be home, others could be work, some may be in public, etc. It's going to be hard keeping everyone's attention, so check out some ways to engage your audience.

1. *Use a PowerPoint presentation.* In many programs you can "share your screen," which means you can choose to share the view of your desktop to your listeners. Use your slides to give more visual input. Don't display all the information at once. If you put it all together on the screen, your audience will see it and assume they have seen the entire presentation. Click the slides as you move through your information so they can see what you're talking about as they hear you. Using engaging and visually attractive graphs and points provide regular visual aids for your viewers.

2. *Use a video to get your viewers involved.* The change of visual aid, and the voice they are hearing, can pull their attention back to the computer screen. There are YouTube videos that you can use to connect with your material. Play a short video that relates to what you're talking about. This is going to be refreshing for your audience, and they are more likely to pay more attention.

3. *Show a website while you are doing your presentation.* Use the "share your screen" feature to pull up a website and demonstrate to your audience. Showing a website helps engage the participants because it changes the view of the content and what is being shared. It also gives the audience an opportunity to complete tasks with you. For example, if you are giving a presentation about language translation, pull up a website to

show your crowd, and have them pull it up at the same time. You run the risk of them not paying attention to you when they pull up the website in their browser. However, you also reap the benefits of engaging them further and allowing them to use the content in real time. The audience will be able to take a break from listening to you speak and can watch you navigate the web browser on your screen as they navigate the browser on theirs. This is going to help your audience remember your presentation better.

4. *Use a cloud sharing document.* You can create a document online that can be shared with other participants and edited in real time. Before the presentation, you can create a blank document and allow open access to your viewers. During your presentation, your audience can use that document to collaborate with you and others. Once the presentation is over, everyone will be able to download a copy and have the digital version to edit. This way, you can get more feedback from your audience.

5. *A poll is a great way to get your audience involved.* You can create a poll or a survey to give your audience during your presentation. Include the poll in your PowerPoint presentation, so while speaking, you can ask them to provide their opinion. This can be something simple as multiple-choice so people can pick the best answer or vote on their choice. You can create a free online survey to have them visit during or after the presentation, you can have them add their answers to the comment section of the shared document, or have them email their answers to you. This is another great way that you can get feedback from your audience, even when you can't see or hear them.

6. *When you start, talk about the importance of the presentation.* Review the important reasons as to why you are speaking today and why it is important for them to listen. Do you want to show them the benefits they are going to gain from your presentation so they will be more engaged during your speech?

7. *Change their visual input.* Science says that listeners can typically drift off after seven minutes. If you keep changing their visual stimuli, it could reset that seven-minute clock. It takes your mind a few moments to process new visual stimuli. Once the brain has understood that stimuli, it moves onto other thoughts. Consistently changing visual stimuli will consistently cause their brain to re-adapt and help them in paying attention in the long-term. (This is actually why most TV shows and movies have a constant frame change. That way we stay interested in what we're watching).

- You start your presentation with your face and the benefits of your speech. Then you move into showing your PowerPoint presentation and pausing to show a website. It's important to occasionally hide the slide shows and show your face on the large screen so you can connect with your audience. Facial expressions are important for you to convey your emotions and message to the audience. Allowing them to see you while you are telling a story or example is going to give them a better connection with you. Don't change the stimulus so much that the audience gets confused. Simply switch screens or slides every couple of minutes to keep your audience engaged.

8. *Turn your camera on.* Even if everyone else has their camera off, make sure yours is on. You are the star of the presentation, and you don't want people staring at a black screen while listening to you talk. Yes, we know it can be nerve-racking, but your presentation is going to be so much better if people can watch you. Otherwise, they are just listening to a podcast.

9. Share a joke or riddle. The joke and riddle will stimulate the minds of your listeners. It involves them in your presentation and if it's good enough it will resonate with them after the presentation. This entertainment can also loosen up the crowd for your presentation.

Chapter Ten: Real-Life

You've covered all the basics. You know everything from what public speaking is to mistakes to avoid. Now you should be ready to apply this book to your real life. In order to be a great public speaker, you need a role model. Luckily, there are many great public-speaking role models you can use as a guide.

Dr. Martin Luther King Jr. is considered one of the best public speakers of all time. With his ability to win over the crowd, he created motivation and inspiration in many listeners. He was able to garner support and start the revolutionary Civil Rights Movement. King used a powerful delivery to convey his message to his followers.

King was a powerful public speaker because he used positivity in his speech. Using positive language can create feelings of inspiration in listeners. Connection was also a large part of King's success as a public speaker. He used his experience as an African American to connect with his audience. This allowed King to create a strong connection with his followers and he built a relationship on this. King used American values, such as freedom and religion, to connect with is audience.

Repetition was also important in King's success as a public speaker. Using a simple, yet powerful phrase to repeat throughout his speech would resonate with the crowd. Using the phrase, "I have a dream," consistently showed his crowd the clarity and importance of his point. The projection he used when speaking showed confidence, which helped him gain credibility with his followers.

King used projection by standing up straight and speaking from the diaphragm. He would plant his feet firmly on the ground and project his voice without straining. Projection is about speaking slowly, loudly, and showing confidence. Some of the greatest aspects about Dr. King as a speaker is that:

- He announced a specific dream.
- He asked for others, not just his children.
- He inspired changed by telling others not to settle for gradual change, but to make change now.
- He didn't use violence or threats.

Another really great speaker is Former President Barack Obama. You can learn a lot about public speaking from seeing Obama's speeches and presentations. Public speaking helped Obama turn into one of the most powerful men in the world. With his ability to win over the crowd, Obama became the first Black president of the United States. Obama is a great public speaker because of his use of stories.

Obama liked to start some of his most important speeches with a story. Stories are so powerful for grabbing your audience's attention. Telling a story to the audience allows them to share emotions with the speaker. They can laugh with us, cry with us, and share our pain. Obama once told the story of an immigrant, as she was standing next to him, when he was fighting with an immigration issue. When he was discussing gun control, he would use recent stories of gun violence.

Eye contact was also a great attribute of Obama's public speaking experiences. He would use eye contact that would make it seem as though he was speaking to each individual person. He speaks with respect- without yelling or being condescending. Obama made it seem like each person in the room was his best friend, and he was only talking to them.

Obama was also really well known for controlling his voice. He used volume, speed, and tone in a normal way. He would alter his voice to fit his speech. Obama would pause to make a point or wait for his audience to finish applause.

His personal life also shows through his speech. He shows his natural side. Being more relatable allows him to create a connection with his crowd. He shows empathy and emotion when appropriate, making him more trustworthy.

One more great public speaking role model is Oprah Winfrey. Winfrey struck the hearts of others with her speech at the Golden Globes after accepting the Cecil B. DeMille Award for lifetime achievement. Winfrey showed the importance of inspiration when public speaking.

Winfrey emphasized action, belief, support, change, feeling, and new thinking. She showed the importance of using these aspects to conjure inspiration in her listeners. Winfrey, like Obama, opened her speech with a story. She immediately wanted to make an emotional connection with the audience.

Because Winfrey made it personal, she created transparency and trust with the crowd. Like King, Winfrey would repeat a strong point to clearly show the crowd her standpoint. She would describe situations in multiple perspectives, repeating herself to make a personal connection with each one of her listeners.

Passion was found throughout Winfrey's speech. She spoke with humility and belief. You could tell that she was discussing her true feelings. She moved her hands and voice with the speech, conveying her emotions.

Her message was clear and powerful. There was no question where she stood on certain topics, and that was evident from her performance. The crowd was able to make such a strong connection because there was no confusion in her message.

The strongest impact of her speech was the very end. A strong closing made her crowd enveloped in the performance. They were energized and excited after the performance. Inspiration would sweep through the crowd as she finished.

Not only are these famous public speakers important, but so are the public speakers in your life. Do you enjoy listening to a preacher preach? Do you like the way a teacher teaches, or the way a student gives a presentation? Find those around you who partake in regular public speaking. Watch their reactions as they move through their speeches. Take notes on what you like about them. Gather skills from them. Be observant and pick up tips that can make you a more comfortable public speaker.

A more informal but still important and influential public speaker is Ellen DeGeneres. While she woos her crowd during every show, she's a great example of being comfortable with yourself and looking to entertain the audience. Ellen regularly discusses important topics on her show, including funding in education, homelessness, and everyday troubles that families and communities face. She uses her platform to give a voice to many people.

Ellen shows passion by engaging with the crowd and using open and happy body language. She laughs often and smiles at the thought of helping others. She seems pleased when she reaches goals on the show and wants the crowd to have fun while seeing her on stage. She definitely leaves a strong impact on her audience and those around her. Ellen is credible, also making her a good public speaker, from her decades of business and acting experience.

Another important public speaker is Greta Thunberg. Greta is most known for skipping school in 2018 to bring awareness to climate change. Greta's vision was to education the world on climate change and how we can work together to change it. She motivated millions of people to join the movement in working for a better climate tomorrow.

Greta is able to connect with her audience using the thoughts of the future. She uses the excitement for tomorrow in her crowd to excel her message. Greta uses emotional appeal to connect with the audience.

Finding a Mentor

Your life, and your public speaking skills, can be completely transformed by a mentor. A mentor is known as an experienced professional who can help guide you in professional goals and opportunities. Not only is it beneficial to have a mentor, but it is also beneficial for the mentor to have a mentee.

It's important to have a mentor that shares the same values as you. When you find someone who shares your values, you can create a stronger bond with them. This strong bond is going to allow you to fully benefit from the relationship and really make a difference in your skills.

Your mentor should be experienced. You need someone who you can go to for advice that is familiar with your topic and your situation. Your mentor should have years of experience in the industry you are pursuing and be able to give you solid and appropriate advice.

A good mentor will be able to lead you to the right answers. You should be challenged by your mentor. A mentor can force you to figure something out while pushing you in the right direction. They help you find yourself within.

Being a mentee allows a mentor to positively affect a life. Having a mentee is very fulfilling in life and provides major satisfaction. They are able to show and expand their leadership skills, while making a friend in the process.

You and your mentor should have a special relationship. This kind of relationship should be built on trust and communication. When looking for a mentor, keep a few things in mind:

1. You want someone you can reach out to often. Long distance may not be an issue as long as you can regularly schedule meetings with them. However, every mentor and mentee relationship is different. You just have to determine what works best with both of your needs and schedules.

2. You want someone who is supportive. Your mentor should be challenging, but it's important for them to still be supportive when you need it. If you don't feel supported by your mentor, then you're less likely to reach out to them with your problems.

3. Define what you want from the mentor relationship. Do you want to network? Do you want them to help you get a promotion, or do you need them to be a reference for you? Make it clear to your mentor what you're looking for. This way they will know what they can do to help you reach your goal. Sharing your goals with them creates a bond you can both benefit from.

4. Keep it causal. You don't have to flat-out ask, "Will you be my mentor?" That puts a lot of pressure on someone and can make them feel obliged to help you. Treat it as a business-friendly relationship.

5. Define your goal. Do you want a promotion? Do you want to land that big client? Find out what you want to do. Then look at the people who are involved. If you want a promotion, try to find a mentor who has been in that job position.

You can reach out to your mentor in times of need. Whether you want advice, a reference, an opinion, or simply the opportunity to discuss your success. You should be able to comfortably talk to your mentor and have no fear expressing your thoughts and concerns.

Example of a Speech

"A student comes to class and sits at their desk. They lay their head down and don't talk much during their class time. They seem to be tired and short tempered with the teacher and the other students.

That next week, the student misses two homework assignments. The student's grade drops a letter due to the missing assignments. The student doesn't seem to show an interest in their grade and doesn't ask to make up the past due work.

The student starts missing class and gaining a lot of absences. When they are in class they are secluded and refrain from any socializing or group work. They don't seem interested in the new material or any extracurriculars around the school.

One day after class the teacher pulls the student to the side and asks them how they've been. They say they've been great and they smile, but the teacher notices that the child's voice is quivering. The teacher realizes something is wrong and comfortably urges them to share what's on their mind. The student shares that they are being bullied and they don't want to come to school anymore.

Being emotionally intelligent means being able to see what's between the lines. An emotionally intelligent person has no problems with understanding the feelings and actions behind others. Having control over your emotions is a big part in emotional intelligence. Understanding when you're feeling anxious or angry and being able to relax yourself and take a break. Being unaware of our emotions can cause us issues at work and in our personal life. When we don't realize we're grumpy, we can be mean to those around us.

Emotional intelligence means expressing emotions at the appropriate time. If we're angry, we shouldn't explode when it's not appropriate. We shouldn't brag and gloat when there are people around us who may be upset from losing. Emotional intelligence consists of recognizing, controlling, and managing our emotions and the emotions of others.

Teachers have a responsibility to be emotionally intelligent. Without emotional intelligence, the teacher wouldn't have been able to see the signs and symptoms of the child being bullied. With no emotional intelligence, the teacher would not have been able to notice that the child was actually upset even though they were saying they were fine.

Teachers need to have emotional intelligence training to help their students, improve education, and increase a positive classroom experience. Teachers can be pivotal mentors in students' lives. When teachers are emotionally intelligent, children feel more comfortable connecting with them and therefore share more of their thoughts and opinions.

When students feel heard, they are more successful in class. Creating an emotional connection through emotional intelligence allows the teacher and student relationship to flourish. When they create a strong relationship, education can be transformed.

With more teachers being emotionally intelligent, education can be changed as we know it. More teachers will be able to realize when children are being bullied. More teachers will be able to understand the problems that students face and be more sympathetic to their situation. Emotional intelligence is going to provide teachers with the ability to help students overcome obstacles and reach their goals in education.

Think of a time when you have had trouble in school. Were you having a problem with an assignment? Did you need advice on a job internship? Were you being bullied, and you needed to reach out for help? Think of the teacher that helped you, if one did. If that teacher helped you, how did they know you needed help? Did you speak to them, or did they reach out to you? Were they able to sympathize with you and offer advice and support?

If you didn't receive any help, or reached out for help and was ignored, think of what could've been better if you had had an emotionally intelligent teacher. What do you think would be different now if you had had a teacher that would've made a difference in your life?

The better the emotional connection between teachers and students, the more positive the classroom experience is going to be. School is a long time for children, and it can get exhausting at times. Students experience problems that teachers cannot understand and that changes as we move through generations.

We all have a class we hate. For some, it's math. Math is my worst subject, and I remember always being frustrated in school. I would sit at the kitchen table for two hours doing simple multiplication problems. I would ask for help from the teacher and my parents because I would struggle with it so bad.

My math teacher was really understanding of this and noticed when I was getting frustrated. When my teacher noticed I was getting upset or obsessing over my work, she would step in and make me feel better. She would walk me through the math and reassure me that it's OK to be confused as long as you work through it and make it out the other side.

School should invest in emotional training for teachers because it can help their students, improve education, and create a positive influence in the classroom."

This is a persuasive speech to try and get schools to invest in emotional intelligence training for teachers. You can see there are three given reasons for the importance of investing in training. There is also no question in what the topic of the essay is about. You can easily understand the topic that the speech is addressing.

This is a strong speech because it starts out with a story. Starting with the story allows you to hook the audience and make them interested in what's going to happen next. It also provides emotional context for the speech, so you have a better understanding of the topic. The speech contains three main reasons that it's important for teachers to gain emotional intelligence training.

The speech is also good because it connects with the audience. It asks them to think of times when they have needed help and times in their past. Having listeners think back on personal experience increases their thoughtfulness. They are mentally pulled into the speech and asked to participate with the speaker.

Personality is shown in the speech when the speaker discusses their experience with a school subject that they had trouble with. They show their weakness to the crowd to improve transparency and credibility.

The speech is also informational because it discusses what emotional intelligence is and how it's important. The reader can understand what emotional intelligence is. This speech uses an emotional appeal to reach out to the audience.

Conclusion

One of the ultimate keys of public speaking is making sure your audience is having a good time. Even if you feel flustered or if you feel like you're doing a bad job, if the audience is enjoying themselves, then you're a good public speaker. The decision ultimately comes down to the audience because they are the ones who determine if you have reached your goal or not. The success of your speech rides on the approval of the audience just as much as the goal. You want people to listen to you because they want to, not because they feel like they have to. Hardly anything will go exactly as planned. You can spend hours and hours of preparation on the presentation, and it still may end in a completely different area than you had hoped or expected. There are lots of problems that can take place while you're giving a public speaking presentation, but it's important to keep your head on straight and move through the speech like you had planned.

As a public speaker, you have to be strong when it comes to criticism. You are always going to have that one heckler, or the person who is going to disagree with everything, or the person who seems to know it all. There are going to be people who are intimidated by you or jealous of you, and that leads to aggression.

Some people may not know if they are intimidating. Others have been told they are intimidating but they cannot recognize it themselves. If you are known to be intimidating, keep that in mind when you are giving a public speaking presentation. If the audience feels intimidated, they can be too focused on their fear, or your intimidation instead of the message you're trying to give.

It's also important not to be too hard on yourself. After all of the information in this book, I'm sure you're racking your brain with everything that could go wrong. You have to remember, though, that you are the one that designed the speech. So, if you forget something or if you mess it up, only you are going to know unless you stop and bring attention to it. If you have a hiccup or leave out an important part of information, you can always say excuse me and continue going.

Being prepared is one of the best ways you are going to be a strong public speaker. Now, some people can improvise really well, so they may not need as much preparation as others. But even the best public speakers still need some preparation. Even those public speakers who have been in the game for decades, topics and audiences are changing every day. Even if you are a master public speaker, it's still important to stay in touch with current public speaking ideas.

Continuing your education as a public speaker takes time and practice. You can practice on your own in the mirror, you can practice with friends and family, you can practice at work with coworkers or your bosses, and you can also attend other speakers' presentations.

When you go to another public speaking presentation, you see things you like and don't like just like your audience.

You can see the way that the audience reacts to that speaker. You can take notes from the point of view as a speaker and also an observant audience member. Being observant is important for being a listener as well as it is for being a speaker.

When you're talking about your presentation, it can be easy to get sidetracked and stop paying attention to your crowd. Being prepared keeps you focused on your content while still being able to focus on your audience because you've practiced. Keeping a focus on your audience is important for ensuring that the entire process moves smoothly.

When you're watching your audience and you see signs of distress, tiredness, or boredom, then you know that you can change and adapt your style to match the room. Even if you had a different plan for the next part of your speech, if you know you need to adapt to the needs of your audience, it's important to make these changes, even if they are on the spot. Don't worry so much about your audience that you forget what you're saying. Perfect your speech behind closed doors so that when it comes time to deliver, you can handle changes that are given to you.

Being a public speaker means being liked by your audience. It also means reaching the goal of your speech. For example, if you are giving a sales pitch, your audience connects with you really well, and they enjoyed your speech, but they aren't buying your product, then your speech may be a failure. Even though you did everything right and your audience had a great time, if they were not motivated to make a sale then it looks like your speech could use some work.

If your goal is to entertain your audience and you simply talk to them without offending them, you may see it as a success because no one was offended. If no one was entertained or laughed throughout the presentation, then it may need help. If you have reached the goal of your speech, then it is successful. Different speeches have different standards for success, so make sure when you go into a public speaking event you know what your goal is. You need to understand what you're working for, so you know what it is going to take to make your speech a success.

This again comes back to being strong when it comes to feedback. Even if you think of the presentation went great, and nothing could've gone any better, but you get poor feedback from your audience, then you need to see it as constructive criticism. It is hard not to take things personal when we are being criticized. Some people may assume that they are being attacked, when in reality, they are simply being offered advice and solutions.

There are also many more important parts to a speech than just the speaker. The speaker can only do so much on their own to ensure a successful speech delivery. If the message is weak or irrelevant, then it could be deemed a bad speech. If the lighting is off, or there is traffic or construction, or a weaker attendance than anticipated, all of these things can contribute to poor public speaking.

If your audience is being inattentive or insulting, it can taint your public speaking performance. There are going to be some circumstances where you are required to public speak in front of an audience that may not necessarily want to be there.

This could be a business proposal with bored coworkers, a class presentation with students who would rather be at home, or in a motivational speech in a jail. It can set you up for failure.

When you are a good public speaker, you are able to garner the attention and respect of your listeners even if they don't want to be there. Many times, you can tell if your listener doesn't want to be at your speech. Their body language and demeanor may give them away. A good public speaker can notice these small acts of rebellion and use them as information to recruit them into what you're saying. If you can adapt your style to their feelings, then you are more likely to give a good public speaking experience for everyone involved, even those who don't want to be there.

It is helpful if you gain the respect from these people who don't want to be here. Your credibility and content can build a base of respect from your audience. You can also look for respect by making eye contact with these people. When you show them that you are strong and confident in yourself then they are more likely to hear what you have to say. You can also re-state why it is so important to hear what you're saying.

Don't be discouraged if you don't feel like an expert public speaker after this book. You still have to practice and get experience to become a good public speaker. But now that you've read this, you have an entire arsenal of tools to help you create, deliver, and execute a successful public speaking experience. After this book you are guaranteed to be a better public speaker. This means you are going to have better experiences with public speaking and continuously get better and better. After a while you still may be nervous before a speech, so don't worry. Just remember your plan and your coping mechanisms to get you on that stage and in front of those people.

Public speaking is about having fun and expressing yourself. You want to use this opportunity to make friends and challenge yourself. Public speaking can provide many opportunities for us in both our personal and professional lives.

Public speaking opportunities can be provided in our personal lives by allowing us to explore our hobbies. We can attend public speaking events that we are interested in and not only learn something new but take notes from the public speaker. It's great if you can attend more public speaking events because you can determine what makes a good speaker and what makes a bad one. You will be able to take notes on what you like and what you don't like.

You will be able to tell not only what you like, but you will be able to observe what the audience is like. You can experience your feelings as an audience member and remember this when you are given your public speaking performance.

Your goal now is to find an opportunity where you can public speak. This doesn't mean go volunteer at a high school to talk about sex ed. You don't even have to talk to more than 10 people. You simply need to find a way where you can put these tips and tricks in place.

While the information is fresh on your mind, challenge yourself to speak in front of others. Volunteer to give a presentation at work. Give a speech at your sister's wedding. Pitch a new product to a few of your friends. Persuade a business and their staff to donate to the local basketball team.

You don't have to start big; you just start where you are comfortable. This may just be practice but you need to practice perfect. Perfect practice makes perfect performance. When you treat a practice performance as though it is extremely important, you're going to get more accustomed to talking about various topics to numerous people. The more do you practice the better you are going to be at becoming a public speaker. You could eventually become someone's mentor.

Take the motivation that you have from this book now and channel it into your career or education. Public speaking can transform all parts of your lives so use this information to make a difference. You can make a difference in your life as well as the lives of others.

Becoming a great public speaker is fulfilling. You can get strong satisfaction from helping others and helping yourself. Public speaking is about what matters to you. Align your public speaking experiences and speeches with your values.

The more involved you are in the presentation the better the chances that you are going to take more from the experience.

Not only do you want to benefit from the experience, but you want others to benefit as well. Encourage those around you to learn more about being a better public speaker, and show them why everyone needs at least a little public speaking skill. Even for people who have never publicly spoken or those that think they never will, having public speaking skills means having good communication skills. Communication is key.

What would be your dream public speaking performance? What is something you are passionate about? What is something you could talk about for hours on end? Do you have a topic that you know a lot about? Do you simply just want to share information with others? If you can answer any of these questions, then you are ready to become a public speaker.

Share your passion and knowledge with the world so it can become a more educated place. Passion and education bring people together and change the world every day. A passion may be hard to find, but once you find yours, you can help others find theirs.